The Beeston *Story*

by
Margaret Cooper

Nottinghamshire **County Council**
Leisure Services

Contents

Introduction

Welcome to Beeston!

The town is situated on the river Trent, 4 miles west of Nottingham. Although it is in close proximity to the city, it has always been strongly independent of it, resisting attempts to become incorporated into it and, through the ages, telling its own distinctive story.

Its geographical setting shows the Tottle Brook forming its eastern boundary; the southern boundary is part of the vast flood plain, and the Bramcote hills form the northern boundary. Between the flood plain and the hills lies an area of terrace gravel which has provided a firm foundation for human settlement from prehistoric times.

Thus we have an ideal situation for the future development of our area which will evolve as our story unfolds.

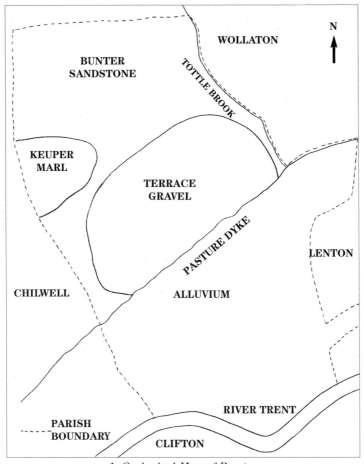

1. Geological Map of Beeston

CHAPTER ONE

Earliest Times

1. Prehistory

You may be surprised to know that the earliest form of primitive man was living in this area from about 80,000 BC to 70,000 BC! This was the time when wild animals, such as the mammoth, woolly rhinoceros, musk-ox and reindeer were roaming amongst the dense forests and grasslands and with which our early ancestors waged constant war they learnt to trap and kill these animals by using simple implements which they made from the flints they found here. They discovered how to chip the flints to produce a sharp edge which could transform a piece of flint into a hand-axe or a chopper.

It was during excavations of the gravel pit in Stoney Street (see fig. 2) in the years from 1897-1909 by Mr. F. W. G. Davey, a keen archaeologist and geologist, that many of these flint tools were discovered. They were grey and heavily rolled as though they had been through water and ice, as indeed they may have been, for they survived the various Ice Ages! This find provided the first indication of the Lower Palaeolithic (Old Stone Age) settlement[1] in the East Midlands and sixty of these implements of unique importance have been deposited in the British Museum where you may see them today. Meantime, workers at the gravel pits at Attenborough have uncovered skeletons or remains of prehistoric animals.

As time went on, these early inhabitants became more advanced - learning to hunt and kill the wild animals with bows and arrows, to use their meat for food which they may have cooked over a fire. The animal skins would provide simple clothing to protect them from the cold. Their flint tools were more sophisticated too, being made from the flakes detached from the

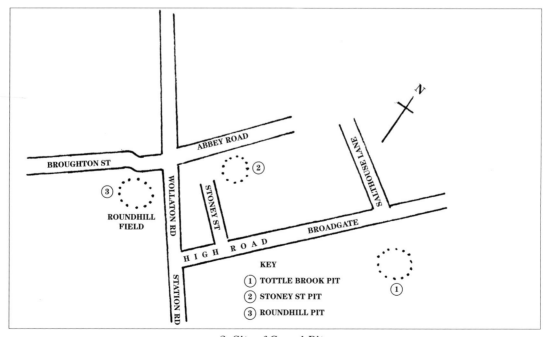

2. Site of Gravel Pits

main flint core and known as *lerallois* flakes, which they could make razor sharp and use as scrapers, hand axes and cleavers – and perhaps as arrowheads – for one has actually been found inside a mammoth! Excavations at the Tottle Brook Pit (situated between Broadgate and Lower Road, see fig. 2) by Mr. Davey disclosed a number of these tools and this proved that these later Stone Age people also lived around here.[2] You may see many of these tools in the

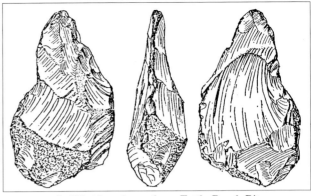

3. Flint hand axe from Tottle Brook Pit

museums at Wollaton Hall, the University and the Castle (see fig. 3). It is also possible that the workmen employed by Sir Louis Pearson, the owner of the Tottle Brook pits, may have some of the tools to show.

It is fair to suppose that this area proved suitable for the later Stone Age (or Neolithic) inhabitants who learnt to farm the well-drained soil after they had cleared some of the forests. By around 4000 BC they had started to lead a more settled life, building their simple huts, fashioning pots from river clay and making more advanced tools from flints, wood and bone.

A prehistoric tool found in West Crescent may date from this period.

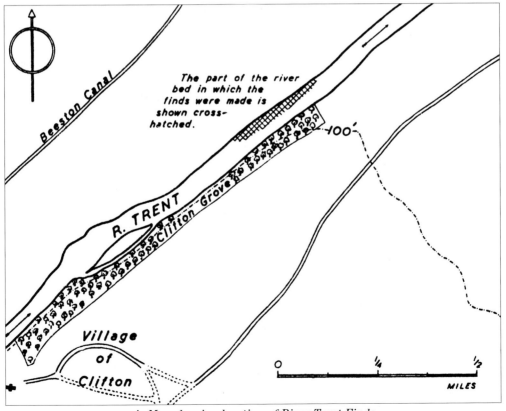

4. Map showing location of River Trent Finds

2. The Bronze Age

By the time of the Bronze Age (4000 to 1000 BC) we are almost certain that there was a settlement by the river. In May 1938, while the river was being dredged, some important finds were made on the Beeston side (see fig. 4) opposite to Clifton Grove.[3] A row of oak stakes set about a yard apart were first discovered in the river bed and then, within this staked area, were found three large dug-out canoes, lying side by

5. Bronze Age canoes

side with bows to the river bank. Two of these, in excellent state of preservation, were able to be rescued and, until recently, were housed in the Castle Museum but are now in the Canal Museum. The other canoe was further out and too decayed to be preserved as it quickly disintegrated when brought to the surface. The boats are of large proportions, 28ft and 30ft long respectively and alike, both being hewn from single oak trunks, hence their name of *monoxylons*, which were hollow when felled and the whole caulked with moss. Experts from the British Museum have considered that they date from the Bronze Age period (see fig. 5). Other finds at the same time in this area seem to confirm this, for there were five large Bronze Age spearheads – one of 22 inches, reputed to be one of the finest in England, together with five smaller spearheads, fragmentary and whole rapiers, swords, knives and a dagger. On the site too, were the skulls of six men, all with holes in the forehead, suggesting their involvement in some skirmish with marauders or enemy tribesmen. It is now believed that the row of stakes found in the river could have been part of a pile structure, possibly a dwelling and that the boats moored there belonged to it. This riverside area was to be of importance for many centuries, as other finds there were to prove.

6. Bronze Age spearheads

Meantime, in November 1978 a Bronze Age pot in perfect condition was discovered in Bramcote - in a site off Cow Lane. Nearby were fragments of a second pot and a collection of cremated bones which belonged to a teenager.[4, 5, 6] The first pot may have contained drink or food as an offering at the burial. It is known that Bronze Age people favoured cremation and their remains were often interred in this type of pot. Archaeologists now wonder if there was a settlement at or near the site.

Outstanding and unique items of bronze tools and weapons have been found in the Attenborough gravel workings, where there was an important settlement. It is believed that this area of the Trent basin carried a population as "intensive and perhaps as rich as anywhere in Bronze Age Britain. It was far from being a backwater!"[5, 6]

3. The Roman Connection

By the time the Romans invaded this country in 43 AD, Nottinghamshire was already inhabited by the Coritani tribe, whose capital was Leicester. As the Roman legions progressed northwards during their first phase of conquest, they recognised the Trent as a natural boundary and established defensive positions along the Fosse Way – including the camp at Margidunum (near Bingham), adopting Leicester or Ratae as they called it, as one of their towns.

7. Mr Harold Hofton with a Bronze Age pot unearthed at Bramcote

Thus, for many years, the land north of the Trent, including Beeston and Nottingham, was largely unaffected by the invasion. It was only after Queen Boudicca (Boadicea) of the Iceni tribe revolted against the Romans about 61 AD and gained help from the Brigantes in Yorkshire and possibly the Coritani, that the Romans decided to push on further north to Yorkshire and eventually to the Scottish border. Some small forts were established in this area though the district was a virtual backwater militarily,[7] but the situation of the camps may have provided useful communication points for the legions.

Recent excavations have provided further information on the sites. Those of special interest to us are the forts at Strutts Park and Little Chester outside Derby,[8] the small fort at Sawley

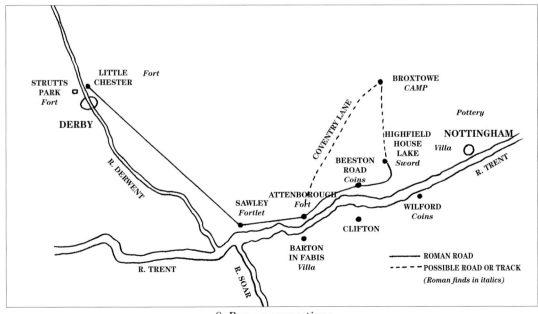

8. Roman connections

9. Roman sword found in Highfield Lake, 1830

(on the field behind the Church) and the fort at Broxtowe[9] (alas! now built over). It seems likely that a road connected the three Derbyshire forts and may have continued to a crossing of the Trent by a ford near Attenborough. Traces of such a road have already been found.[10]

In later years the Romans established civilian settlements and villas nearby. Across the river, villas have been located at Barton and Red Hill at Thrumpton.[11] In 1834 remains of such a villa were discovered near Highfield House and a Romano-British sword was found in the lake there.[12] Just recently a Roman coin was picked up close by the house, one in Lenton Abbey Estate, another on Derby Road, and others were found by the river when the Bronze Age canoes were unearthed.

In 1849 we are told that a Roman road was discernible here and an ancient building.[13] The road mentioned may have been a continuation of the road from Derby to Sawley and Attenborough, which would extend to the villa at Highfield House and thence to Broxtowe. A later writer suggests that this road would come through the fields via Long Lane and the line of the present Queen's Road (or Middle Pasture Road as it was called) up Hassocks Lane and across the fields to Highfield House[14] and thence to the Broxtowe camp (opposite Broxtowe Hall Close in Nottingham) which is in direct line with it. Another ancient road – probably a British trackway originally – came from the ford at Attenborough and went due north to reach Coventry Lane and thence to Broxtowe. So it is almost certain that the early British inhabitants of Beeston would see Roman soldiers and civilians as they made their way through this area.

Sources (Chapter One)
[1]*Proceedings of the Prehistoric Society*, (1963); Merrick Posnansky, *Lower and Middle Palaeolithic Industries of the East Midlands no. 12*; *East Midland Archaeological Bulletin*, (1973)
[2]*Proceedings of the Prehistoric Society*, (1963); Merrick Posnansky, *Lower and Middle Palaeolithic Industries of the East Midlands no. 12*, *East Midland Archaeological Bulletin*, (1973)
[3]J.W. Phillips F.S.A., Recent Finds in the Trent near Nottingham, *Antiquaries' Journal* April 1941
[4]Report in *Nottingham Evening Post*, 15 November, 1978
[5]Report of lecture by Mr. Jeffrey May, Head of Archaeological Department, University of Nottingham, June 1979
[6]Report of Interview with Mr. Jeffrey May, July 1979
[7]*Origins of Britain*, p.56
[8]Tom Garlick, *Roman Derbyshire* (1975), pp.35-8, 42
[9]A.C. Wood, *History of Nottinghamshire*, p.5
[10]Lewis, *Topographical Dictionary of England*, (1849)
[11]*Victoria County History, Nottinghamshire Vol 2*, p.23
[12]Godfrey, *History of the Parish of Lenton*, p.16
[13]Lewis, *Topographical History of England*, (1892)
[14]Godfrey, *History of the Parish and Priory of Lenton*, pp.13-4

CHAPTER TWO

The Saxon Village

1. The Saxon Settlement

With the collapse of the Roman Empire and the withdrawal of the Romans from Britain in 410 AD, the Britons were left in a relatively defenceless position and a prey to marauding tribes of Picts and Scots. At the same time, the Angles, Saxons and Jutes from the Schleswig Holstein area of Germany were being forced from their homes by the Danes and were making their way to England where our land promised greater fertility.

During the sixth and seventh centuries the Angles sailed up the river Trent under cover of darkness as pirates, attacking the little British settlements and establishing themselves in the Nottinghamshire, Lincolnshire and Derbyshire areas. By 584 AD Nottinghamshire was marked as the home of the Middle Angles. As they were primarily agricultural people, they were looking for suitable conditions in which to set up their farming communities.

Here, around Beeston, they found an almost ideal site. By the river, the ground had been cleared by the earlier Bronze and Iron Age settlers to reveal lush green meadows and fields with rye (or the bent grass) growing wild. Above the flood plain was shorter grass for all the year round pasturage, and gravel terraces – roughly on the line of Nether Street and Middle Street, which would provide a firm foundation for their simple wooden houses, without diminishing the area of agricultural land available. Beyond this, the higher ground sheltered by the sandstone hills of Bramcote could be utilised for their seasonal crops. Clear pure water seeped down through the bunter sandstone to provide a good supply for man and beast.

With these obvious advantages, it is not surprising that family groups of Angles decided to make their homes here and thus to found the village. We have evidence of their presence here in the fine Anglo-Saxon shield boss and the plain cruciform fibula (clasp) which were found in the Trent near the Bronze Age canoes. These may be seen in the Castle Museum.

In due time, the village was given the name of *Bes-tun*, meaning in Saxon the 'tun' or settlement of 'bes' - the bent or rye grass. How appropriate this choice of name must have been, for to find such a crop growing wild must have seemed wonderful to them! Today, the area by the river, where you may still see rye growing wild, is called the Ryelands and older folk can remember the fields of rye on Trent Road.

Having cleared the higher ground above the gravel terraces, the Angles were able to set up their traditional method of open field farming, using the two large fields for their winter and spring sowing crops, while the third field stood fallow and was left for the grazing of the animals. Each year, the crops and the fallow land was rotated so that the soil could be renewed and fertilised by the animal manure.

Here in Beeston we are able to trace the location of the fields, the common pasture and the meadow land beyond, for much of these early land arrangements continued until the eighteenth and early nineteenth century. The two large arable fields lay above the gravel terraces (ie above Middle Street) and were separated by a rough track probably worn by the cattle as they came to graze on the fallow field. This track was on the line of Wollaton Road, and the arable fields lay east and west of this. The East or Tottle Brook field stretched along the present High Road and Broadgate to the Tottle Brook, thence by the brook to Derby Road and to the Wollaton Road junction. The West or Church field went along Chilwell Road to the boundary by the Hop Pole Inn and up to Derby Road and along to the Wollaton Road junction. The third field lay between the gravel terrace and the river, including the Ryelands and part of the land taken up by the Cliftonside estate. This was designated as the Nether (or lower) field. The remaining land was meadow and pasturage for common use.

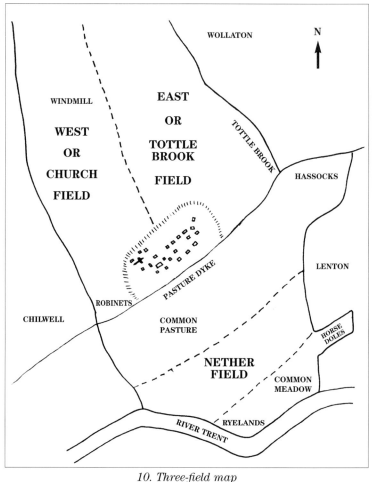

10. Three-field map

The settlement, comprising a large wooden thatched roofed house for the leader or chief, with some smaller houses for his followers, would have been in the area covered by Middle Street (eastern section), Nether Street and the City. It would be enclosed by a high wooden fence or stockade as a defence against intruders. Small streams of pure water ran through the settlement from the sandstone hills beyond. These were later connected to form the Pasture Dyke. This dyke, though now culverted, can be traced and provides a good guide to the boundary of the village houses as it existed for many centuries. It runs from the Robinets in the west, through the Community Centre grounds, under Dovecote Lane just beyond Dovecotes, across to Station Road by the premises of Foster & Pearson, thence below Nether Street and the back of the John Clifford school to the City, by the back of the Day Centre and Humber Lodge, under Humber Road, beside Fletcher Road and the footpath to Queen's Road, where it joins the Tottle Brook.

All the villagers were freeholders of part of the land, except for any captured Britons who may have been kept as slaves by the chieftain. The villagers would be allocated strips of land in each of the fields as well as grazing rights in the common meadow and pasture lands. The primitive unit of land division was the tenement of a normal peasant, the holding of which supported the

11. Reconstruction of a Saxon hut

villager (or Ceorl) and his household; this was a hide, whose acreage varied. The maximum holding for a ceorl was five hides.

The wooden Anglo-Saxon plough – an essential implement for land cultivation – was heavy and unwieldy, often requiring eight oxen to pull it, so the villagers would band together to obtain the equipment. The strips, generally 22 yards wide and 220 yards long, were planned for the convenience of these implements and were separated by earthen mounds called baulks. Baulk Lane at Bramcote is a reminder of these divisions. Each villager had to erect wattle fencing around his strips to protect them from stray animals during the growing time. The chief crops here were oats, rye and barley, together with beans, peas and lentils.

All the men of the village and boys over the age of 14 years had a voice in the village council or moot, which would be held from time to time to elect representatives to the Hundred or Shire Moot, which would be held at Broxtowe, and to make important decisions on village affairs. Meantime, by the seventh century England was divided into various kingdoms. The Midland area was called Mercia (from the Saxon 'Mierce' meaning the Boundary Folk) and Beeston was included in North Mercia, under King Penda.

2. The Coming of Christianity

At first the Anglo-Saxons continued their worship of heathen gods - Thor, Woden, etc., but the influence of Christian missionaries from Ireland and Iona to Northumbria and from Rome with Augustine to Kent in 597 AD and Paulinus to North Nottinghamshire about 604 AD meant that around 655 AD[1] the people of our area were converted to Christianity.

Two monasteries were established in adjoining counties: one at Repton about 630 AD and another at Breedon-on-the-Hill about 675 AD,[2] and it is possible that monks from these places would travel on foot around the

12. The Breedon Angel, Breedon-on-the-Hill Parish Church

9

13. Stapleford Cross

district preaching and teaching. It is known that from 691-702 AD St. Wilfrid was living in Mercia under the protection of King Aethelred and founded many monasteries in the kingdom.[3] He was a passionate evangelist as well as a great statesman and must have had a profound influence over the whole area. It is possible that Wilford, as "Wilfrid's Ford" may have been connected with him.

We have definite evidence of Christian worship in Anglo-Saxon times in this district by the fine Saxon preaching cross which is to be seen in the churchyard at Stapleford today.[4] It was around this that people would gather to listen to the good news of the Gospel proclaimed by the local priest or travelling monk, long before a church was built in their village. At Attenborough, it is believed that a holy man or hermit called Edda or Adda had his cell, hence its Saxon name of Adenburgh.[5] In later Saxon times, a church was to be built there to serve the villages of Chilwell and Toton.[6]

Thus we may assume that the people of Bestune too became Christians during the seventh and eighth centuries, though we have no record of a church here until much later.

3. The Danish Invasions - and Beeston under the Danelaw

The eighth and ninth centuries saw the peaceful life of Anglo-Saxon Beeston frequently disturbed by Danish pirates who sailed down the Trent by night, raiding villages and burning and looting the wooden houses. It is easy to believe that the inhabitants' fervent prayer at this time was:

"From the assaults of the Vikings, Good Lord, deliver us"

Later they would hear of, or even see, some of the great Danish army which came down from their headquarters in York and encamped outside Nottingham on St. Mary's Hill in 868 AD. They remained there for two years and at last, Burrhead, the King of Mercia, appealed to and gained help from Aethelred, King of Wessex and his brother, Alfred (who later became King Alfred). They came to Nottingham with their army, perhaps passing through Beeston en route. They besieged the Danish fortifications until peace was made and the enemy returned to York in 870 AD. Alas! this was not the end of the matter, for in 874 AD the Danes came down the Trent, no doubt via Beeston and encamped at Repton that winter and where today archaeological evidence of their presence has been found.[7] By 877 Nottingham, Derby, Leicester, Stamford and Lincoln were all in the hands of the Danes. Only King Alfred and his army in Wessex had withstood the enemy, who were defeated at the battle of Ethandune. Their leader, Guthrum, assented to the peace treaty of Wedmore in 878, was baptized as a Christian and promised that his followers would live here peaceably.

As a result, Alfred gave the Danes settlement rights in Bedfordshire, Huntingdonshire, Northamptonshire, Leicestershire, Nottinghamshire, Derbyshire and Lincolnshire; and the Five Boroughs of Nottingham, Derby, Leicester, Stamford and Lincoln which became known as the Danelaw.

Beeston was firmly included in this, and as a result various changes were seen here:

1. The Danish language appears to have been introduced; with field names of Scandinavian origin existing here for centuries; some were found on the Tithe Award Map of 1806. The chief were *Glead Wong* ('wong' was Scandinavian for a meadow); *Musco Syke* ('syke' was Scandinavian for a small stream); *Heanings* (Scandinavian term) and *Geta* (Scandinavian for a road or street).

14. England after Alfred's peace with the Danes

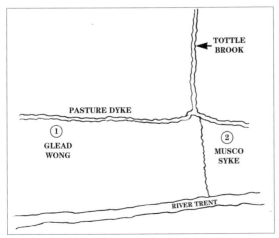

15. Danish names found in use on Tithe Award map, 1806

2. The Danish land measures were adopted – as a result: *Carucates* (of approximately 120 acres) were used instead of the Anglo-Saxon 'hides'.

3. The Saxon Moot which was held at Broxtowe now became the *Wapentake of Broxtowe*. This name 'Wapentake' was the Scandinavian name meaning 'weapon brandishing', from the custom of members of the assembly touching the upheld spear of the Headman as a sign of common and united interest and the promise of good conduct.

4. Troubled Times of the Tenth and Eleventh Centuries

After the death of King Alfred in 901 AD, his successor Edward the Elder decided to gain control of Mercia for the Saxons. He and his sister, Aethelfloed, Lady of the Mercians, with their armies, advanced against the Viking armies of the East Midlands. A fortress was built at Tamworth (the remains of which can still be seen) and this, together with the fortified burghs of Derby, Leicester,

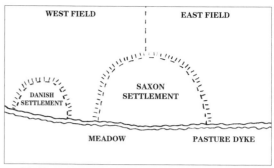

16. Danish and Saxon settlements in Beeston

Nottingham, Stamford and Lincoln, formed a strong base for attack, with the result that the whole area was taken over by the Saxons. King Edward himself conquered Nottingham in 918-9, bridging and fortifying the Trent crossing and ordering the building of a wall around the town in 920.

In 921-2 Edward came to Tamworth and having received the submission of the people of that area, moved on to Nottingham. He must have passed through Beeston on this journey, and we can imagine how delighted the inhabitants would have been to see the King and his retinue. On arrival in Nottingham, he had the town garrisoned and repaired by the English and the Danes, and proceeded to order the building of a fort on the south bank of the Trent (at West Bridgford). By 922 AD the whole of Mercia was in his possession and all the people both English and the Danes submitted to him.

In 924 AD Edward came from Nottingham to Bakewell and probably passed through the north of Beeston on his way. The King died in 925 AD and was succeeded by his son, Athelstan, who again found it necessary to fight against the Danes. In 930 AD he held a *Witanagemot* in Nottingham. This was an assembly of his wise men and counsellors and included three Welsh princes, the Archbishop, sixteen bishops, thirteen dukes, twelve thanes and twelve untitled persons. These representatives would travel from all over the country to Nottingham and the folk of Beeston would certainly have seen some of them as they made their way to the meeting place. After Athelstan's death, his son Edmund eventually brought the Danes under submission in this area in 942 AD, and the two races seemed to have settled down amicably here, though the country itself had a century of unsettled rule with weak Saxon kings and strong Danish kings such as Sweyn and Canute.

During the tenth and early eleventh centuries, groups of Danish agriculturalists came over peaceably to settle here. They would be given the right to live in unallocated lands outside the bounds of the existing village. These men would be freer than the other villagers in that the land would be their own and they would not be required to give so much service to the thane or lord, only loyalty and service to the king. These men were called *soc* or *soke men*. We know from the Domesday Book that by 1065 we had at least one soc man living in Beeston. By this time too, the village had been divided into three manors or estates, each with their own thane or lord. Prior to the Norman Conquest, they were Alfag, Alwine and Ulchel. It may be that these three were related and that one took the main responsibility. It is almost certain that the village constituted a single unit for taxation and other purposes.

It would be usual for the thane to have his own house or hall on his estate, but we have no actual evidence of the position of these halls. One may have been in the City, another on the site of the present Manor House and the third at West End near the Robinets. Ulchel is mentioned in the Domesday Book as holding lands in Bramcote and Clifton, so it is possible that his estate in Beeston could have been contiguous with the Bramcote land, ie on the West End of the village. Alfag held land in the Basford area too, so his holding here may have been on the east side, with Alwine holding the central area.

The soc man's holding could have been on the west side near to the Chilwell boundary: an area outside the original settlement. The villagers with their families would be clustered around central Middle Street and Nether Street areas where traces of their small holdings could be seen on the Tithe Award Map of 1806.

Sources (Chapter Two)
[1]*Anglo-Saxon Chronicle for 655 AD*
[2]*Anglo-Saxon Chronicle for 675 AD*
[3]The Venerable Bede, *Ecclesiastical History*
[4]Stenton, *Anglo-Saxon England*, p.143
[5]Arthur Cossons, *Beeston and Stapleford Guide*
[6]*Domesday Book*
[7]Press Report, 5 September, 1986

CHAPTER THREE

Medieval Beeston

1. The Norman Conquest and the Domesday Survey

On the death of Edward the Confessor in January 1066, his cousin Duke William of Normandy declared himself heir to the English throne. Meantime, the Witanagemot (Saxon Parliament) chose Earl Harold, King Edward's brother-in-law to succeed. William, determined to secure his rights, took advantage of Harold's absence in the north to invade in the south. Both armies eventually met at Senlac Hill outside Hastings on 14th October, 1066, where a bitter battle ensued in which Harold and many of his men were killed. William then advanced towards London where he was crowned in Westminster Abbey on Christmas Day 1066.

The country as a whole did not accept William for some time. There were rebellions in Yorkshire and East Anglia especially. We are told "the invasion was fiercely opposed by the inhabitants of Nottingham, but after much bloodshed they were obliged reluctantly to capitulate".[1]

2. Beeston after the Conquest

After William I's visits to this area in 1068 and 1069, en route for Yorkshire to quell the rebellions there, the allocation of lands to his followers would begin. Between 1066 and 1075 there was an almost complete transfer of land from the English and Scandinavian lords to the Norman tenants-in-chief. William Peveril, reputed stepson of the King, had already been ordered to build the Castle in Nottingham on the great rock in 1068 and it would be no surprise that he was granted the Governorship of it, together with land and 60 houses in the town. In addition, he received 66 manors in Nottinghamshire, some in Derbyshire and Bedfordshire; 162 in all.

Among these was the multiple manor of Bestune, formerly owned by Alfag, Alwine and Ulchel. It is just possible that these three thanes may have continued to hold their estates as sub-tenants, paying rent and service for the privilege. The soc-man would provide rent and fealty

17. Beeston's entry in the Domesday Book, 1086

as he had done in King Edward's time. According to the Domesday Book entry there were 17 villeins (or villagers) occupying land here and giving service and fealty to Peveril. This gives us some evidence of the population at that time. Considering the number of villeins with their wives and families, and the bond servants of the lord, this could probably amount to between 70 and 80 persons.

The Domesday survey of 1086, while giving us important facts of land ownership, was compiled primarily as an estimate of the taxation yields of the various estates in the country and not as an exact account of the acreage and extent of an estate. Nottinghamshire as a border county had, for centuries, been lightly taxed in view of the fact that it must be prepared at short notice to repel invaders from the north. This policy seems to have been continued under William I. As a result, Beeston was tax rated at 3 carucates (approximately 360 acres) although its actual acreage was 1,500 acres. One interesting fact from the Domesday Book entry is the 24 acres of meadow land mentioned. From a study of the Saxon allocation of meadow land here, it is easy to realise that the meadow land was more extensive than this. But the Horse Doles meadow on the eastern corner of the village is approximately 24 acres in extent. We know from the Accounts Roll of 1297 that this area was treated separately for tithes and it may be that from 1086 it was enclosed and held in severalty: hence its special mention. The taxation yield of 30 shillings, both in Edward the Confessor's time and in William I's suggests that the estate was unchanged in extent and cultivation.

We have no knowledge of William Peveril visiting his manor here – the estate would have been managed by his steward or bailiff – but he must have passed through the village to and from his journeying to his estates in Derbyshire, one of which was Castleton, where the remains of his great Peveril Castle still stand. He founded two institutions, however, which were to have an effect on Beeston. One was the manorial court called the 'Honour of Peveril' which had extensive jurisdiction in 127 villages in Nottinghamshire, including Beeston; 120 in Derbyshire and others in Yorkshire and Leicestershire. This court was almost as important as a royal court dealing with serious offences until 1316. It probably held its proceedings in the Chapel of St. James on Friar Lane. Eventually it became a Debtor's Court and was located in the White Hart Inn on Gregory Street, Lenton, until it was closed in 1849. We are fortunate to have records of this court which provide information about the people of the village through the centuries.

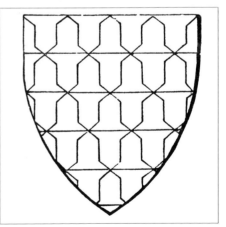

18. Arms of the Peveril family

Peveril was very conscious of the need to provide for his eternal well-being and to this end he allocated land in Lenton for the building and establishing of a Cluniac priory there between 1103 and 1108. Here the monks would pray continually for the souls of himself and his family. By the royal charter of Henry I, the Priory was dedicated to the Holy and Undivided Trinity. It was splendidly endowed by Peveril and many other noblemen who gave land, churches and tithes from places far and near, so that it became one of the wealthiest priories in the country. The Norman font from the Priory is still to be seen in Lenton parish church. Beeston was to become very much involved with the Priory after the death of Peveril and his sons, as later chapters will show.

19. Arms and Seal of Lenton Priory

Meantime, the Peveril family continued to hold the manor here through the reigns of William I, William II and Henry I. Then came the turbulent reign of Stephen (1135-54) when civil war erupted after Henry's death due to the rival claims of Henry's daughter, Matilda. William Peveril II remained firmly in support of Stephen and during the war saw Nottingham severely damaged by Matilda's forces. In the end, Matilda's son, Henry, finally defeated Stephen's army and was proclaimed King as Henry II. Peveril fled from Nottingham and took sanctuary in the Priory, and as a result he and his family were deprived of all their estates.

Thus Beeston and all the other manors came into the possession of King Henry in 1154. This was important for Beeston, as royal manors had special concessions, such as exemption from certain taxes, which once given, were rarely repealed. For seventeen years, until 1171, Beeston remained in royal possession. Then changes took place which were to affect Beeston for many centuries. (See Appendix 1 and Appendix 2 on page 83 for the full lists of the Lords of the Manor up to 1537).

3. The Church

Although a church is not mentioned in the Domesday Book entry, it is almost certain that there would have been a place of worship here from Saxon times. In Norman times it was usual for a church to be built by a layman, generally the Lord of the Manor within his own

20. Conjectural Illustration of Lenton Priory, as viewed from the north-east

demesne and as his own property. As such, he claimed the right to appoint his own chaplain as priest. It is possible that William Peveril or his successor had a church built here, probably on the same site, which would be within the lord's demesne.

The first definite evidence of a church here is in 1171, when the priest (name unknown) and church wardens took the Pentecostal offerings of 1s 8d to Southwell Minster. Southwell had been nominated as the Mother Church of the diocese, and at Pentecost each parish had to bring its offerings for the upkeep of the Minster, and would receive in return a supply of holy oil for the next year. The amount of Beeston's offering gives us a clue as to the population then, for the 1s 8d represented the tax imposed on each household by the church. It was customary for this to be based on the number of chimneys or smoke holes each house possessed, each one being taxed at $\frac{1}{4}$d and commonly referred to as 'smoke farthings'. Assuming that most houses had only one chimney, this amount (1s 8d) would represent a total of 75-80 houses, the Manor house possibly having more chimneys than the rest. This would give a village population of 250-300, and an increase on the Domesday estimate.

Nothing more is heard of church affairs until about 1200 when Robert, a chaplain, is mentioned, and about 1240 when Roger, a clerk of Beeston, witnessed a deed. Both these men may have been lay clerks or monks in the service of the lord of the manor or the Priory at Lenton.[2]

From about 1160, Lenton Priory had appealed to the Popes Alexander III and Lucius III for permission to appropriate certain churches and their tithes to gain endowments for its upkeep.[3] As a result, Beeston church was duly appropriated despite the protestations of its parishioners, and it became a chapel under the Priory, who gained the advowson or right to appoint a vicar. In addition, the sum of 22 shillings each year was claimed by the Priory from the vicar whose income from the vicarage was only £5 6s 8d! The Priory retained the advowson and appropriate tithes until the Dissolution of the monasteries in 1537. The Priory arms are still to be seen on the outside of the east end of the present church as a reminder of the Priory's long connection with the parish.[4]

In September 1267 the first vicar, John de Brademore, was appointed and ordained deacon in 1268. He was followed by Matthew de Leycestre in 1275.[5] We have one relic from this thirteenth century church: the top part of the font, which was found buried under the altar when the church was rebuilt in 1843. (See Appendix 3 on page 84 for other vicars of Beeston between 1200 and 1485).

11th February, 1300/1 must have been a red letter day in Beeston for, on that day, the Archbishop of York, Archbishop Corbridge, with his train of monks and clerics paid an episcopal visitation en route from Felley Priory to Lenton Priory.[6] Alas! we have no other record of the visit but it must have caused a stir as the procession on horseback rode to church for Mass and then passed on through the meadows to Lenton where the prior and convent would be waiting to greet them. This was indeed an occasion to be remembered by the inhabitants for many years to come!

In 1327 Matthew de Leycestre was succeeded by William de Willesthorpe, and it was during his time that a dispute arose with the Priory over the repair of the chancel and the annual

21. The Font, Beeston Church

payment of 22 shillings by the vicar and parishioners.[7] No doubt the cost of the repair would have been well above the means of the villagers and the added burden of the 22 shillings annually would have presented them with an impossible situation. Consequently, the matter was brought before two commissioners, the Rector of Arnold, John de la Launde, and William de Hundon, Rector of Barmborough, Yorkshire. We have no definite information as to the result, but it would appear that the Priory claimed the vicarage tried to evade its duty to repair the chancel and to insist on the vicar paying the 22 shillings to the Priory, when the total income of the vicarage was only £5.6s.8d.

The fact that for centuries tithes and other monies belonged to Lenton Priory and they had the right of advowson explains why Beeston had a vicar rather than a rector. However, a few years after, political matters were to bring changes in the Priory's authority, as later chapters will show.

4. The Manors

In 1171 Henry II, who had held the manor since 1154, granted the greater part of it to Hugh de Beauchamp, Baron, of Eaton Socon, Bedfordshire[8], who was of some importance at court apparently, for in 1176 he was chosen to accompany Henry II's daughter to Palermo, where the marriage with the King of Sicily had been arranged.[9] In 1186 Beauchamp went on a pilgrimage or a crusade to the Holy Land and was presumed to have died there. However, he eventually returned and died in 1216.[10] He was succeeded by his brother, Roger, and the estate was held by the Beauchamp family and their descendants until the mid fourteenth century.

A small part of the Manor was granted at the same time, ie 1171, to Adam de Argenteon of Wymondley, Hertfordshire. He in turn gave the land to Wymondley Priory, which had been founded by his relative, Richard de Argenteon. It is possible that this land was that part of Beeston which had originally been held by the Danish soc man, and would be clearly definable as being that area away from the original Saxon settlement. It was to be known as the Monastic Manor and the Prior of Wymondley was Lord of the Manor there. However, it was soon realised that the two manors could not be organised separately, and by 1216 Hugh de Beauchamp was given the overlordship of the priory land. The monastic manor had the greater continuity of tenure under successive priors and its tenancy being let out to farmers at a rental, remained until the Dissolution of the monasteries in 1537. By the end of the fifteenth century the Beauchamp manor was held by three sub-tenants who were descendants of the original family.

21a. Seal of Wymondley Priory

As the Beauchamps owned manors in other parts of the country, it is doubtful if they ever resided in a manor house here, and this manor would have been entrusted to a steward, who would have been responsible for supervising the estate and presiding over the manorial court. It is just possible that the Prior of Wymondley may have visited his Beeston estate from time to time and stayed at a house on his land here, hence our two manor houses today.[11] Credence for this is lent by the fact that a Roger de Beeston was Prior of Wymondley from 1349-74.[12]

The Organisation of the Manors in Beeston

In the Middle Ages, 'the manor' meant an estate which was an economic unit in which all the tenants were bound to the lord and his demesne farm; the free tenants paying his rent for their land and helping him at busy seasons; the unfree tenants doing weekly labour, service, and all of them regularly attending his manorial court for the settlement of quarrels and the regulation of communal affairs.[13]

Many villages had the Lord of the Manor and his family residing in the village, eg at Clifton and Strelley. Beeston was in a different situation, as from 1216 the overlordship of the village was granted to the Beauchamp family, while acknowledging the Prior of Wymondley as the holder of the monastic manor. Thus it was possible for Beeston to be organised as one entity, probably under a salaried Steward or Bailiff, acting on behalf of the lord of the manor, and who would have general oversight and responsibilities for the manorial court. But the principal responsibility for the manorial work commonly rested with the Reeve, who would be elected annually by the villeins from their number. His job was to organise the work to be done on the lord's demesne, to see that the servants carried out their various duties each day and to arrange the 'week work' to be undertaken by the villeins. This 'week work' was the manual labour required of each tenant by the lord of the manor, and this was usually light in Nottinghamshire. The Reeve might also be required to collect the rents from the 'soc' men and other tenants. In return for these duties, he was exempt from other service and rents to the lord and may have received food and other perquisites from him. The Reeve's position was an onerous one involving not merely the organisation of labour and rent collection, but often the buying and selling of animals and produce, the upkeep of farm buildings and implements, and at the end of the year he had to account for the proceeds of the manor. A thirteenth century treatise giving advice on the election of a reeve said: *"No Reeve ought to remain longer than one year unless he has proved himself very capable, just in his actions and well able to further his lord's interests."* The Reeve had the power to appoint a Hayward to supervise the gathering of the harvest, but the manor's lands and property also required the services of others.

Sources (Chapter Three)
[1]Robert Mellors, *In and about Nottinghamshire*, p.34
[2]Robert Mellors, *Beeston Then & Now*, p.5
[3]Middleton Papers, pp.41 & 63
[4]Deverill, *History of the Parish Church*
[5]ibid
[6]York Registry (Archbishop Corbridge), p.182
[7]Deverill, *History of the Parish Church*, p.23
[8]Dugdale, *Baronetcy*
[9]*Victoria County History, Bedfordshire*
[10]*Red Book of Exchange and Pipe Rolls*
[11]*Victoria County History, Bedfordshire*
[12]Ecclesiastical references
[13]Steaton, *Middle Ages*, p.133

CHAPTER FOUR

William de Beckford –
King's Clerk

In 1337 war with France (later to be called the Hundred Years War) began. As a security measure King Edward III took over all alien monasteries and convents in England. Amongst these was the Cluniac Priory of Lenton, which had particularly close links with its mother house of Cluny in France. As we know, Lenton Priory had responsibility for presenting a priest at Beeston and so this duty now fell to the King. Consequently, on the death of the vicar here, William de Willesthorpe in 1339, Edward took the opportunity to appoint one of his own clerks, William de Beckford, who was also an ordained priest, to the living here.

There were probably two reasons for the King's decision - firstly because he may have wished to pension off William from his service and yet ensure him an adequate living; and secondly and more importantly, Edward wished to have a shrewd representative in the area who could be in close touch with the Priory and its affairs and able to report on any matters which seemed suspect.[1] In short, he was to be the King's Private Eye in Lenton!

William de Beckford was duly instituted to the vicarage on 20th June, 1339 but it was soon obvious that his appointment was distasteful to the Prior of Lenton, especially as the King had also granted to William the right of corrody at the Priory.[2] This right was a grant for life – confirmed on 3rd October, 1341 – of a daily subsistence of a white loaf and a gallon of the best ale for himself and a loaf and a gallon of second quality ale for his servant, or he could have a

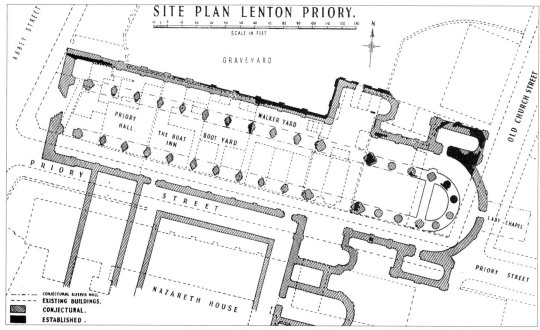

22. Site plan of Lenton Priory

penny a day for himself and a halfpenny for his servant. Annually he was to receive a clerical robe or a mark (13s 4d) in money, while his servant was to receive a robe like the Prior's servants or half a mark. At Martinmas, William was to have two cartloads of sea coal and wood, together with four pounds of candles. This was in addition to his normal dues as vicar, which in 1340 were over £10! (ie 1/9 of the wool tithe £8, rent from 32 acres of Glebe Land £1 9s 6d, small tithes 14s 6d and tithes of hay 10s 0d).

It is hardly surprising, therefore, that Astorgius the Prior appears to have disputed the King's nomination of William and to have made life rather unpleasant for him. However, this matter was reported to the King who proceeded to issue a further order on 9th December, 1340[3] prohibiting all ecclesiastical persons from proceedings in derogation of the King's late presentation of William de Beckford, King's Clerk to the Church at Beeston.

Further sanctions were also applied to the Prior for in 1342,[4] the King confirmed that Astorguis was permitted to hold the Priory, but at a rent of 100 marks per year! Among the mainpernots or guarantors for the annual payment of this sum was William de Beckford. This seems to confirm the view that William was to act as the King's agent on Priory matters. Indeed, on the death of Astorgius in 1349 (probably from the plague) William, together with Vincent de Fescampo the sub-prior and William de Valeys, one of the monks, became joint keepers of the Priory until a successor was appointed.[5]

Some months after this, William resigned from his living here on his appointment as Chapter Clerk at Lincoln.[6] But his interest in this area continued, for in February 1350 the new Prior of Lenton, finding some difficulty in collecting his farms' rents, tithes and pensions, appointed William and three others to collect the arrears due to the Priory. In recognition of this service, the Prior and Convent leased to William for life the tithe sheaves of Beeston, the Grange (tithe barn) there and their share of the tithes of Attenborough, Chilwell and Toton.[7] In return for this concession, William agreed to pay the Priory 84 qtrs. of corn to be handed over at Beeston at times to suit the convenience of the Prior and Convent. This fixed payment was to comprise 42 qtrs. barley, 21 qtrs. peas, 4 qtrs. wheat and 8.5 qtrs. rye and drag cleaned and winnowed.[8] This gives some knowledge of the main crops grown here. William was also to have for life the lease of a plot of meadow in Lenton called 'Lytel Lything' in lieu of the robes for himself and his servant (valued at 13s 4d and 6s 8d) which were due to him under the terms of the corrody. He also remitted the arrears of the 20 shillings payment in exchange for the tithes of Attenborough, Chilwell and Toton.

In 1352 William de Beckford, now known as William de Beston, returns to Nottinghamshire as

Rector of Cotgrave[9] and in November 1352 he remembers his old parish of Beeston and decides to seek the King's permission to found a chantry chapel there. This was readily given.[10] It was during Edward III's time that the church here was rebuilt and it could have been about this time, which would encourage William to make his proposal. We have three important relics from this fourteenth century church incorporated into the present building. They are the image niche on the north side of the east window, the piscina and the double sedilia on the south side of the

23. *Double sedilia and piscina, Beeston Church*

chancel. The fact that the sedilia is a double one suggests that the church must have been quite important, with seats for the priest and the sub-priest officiating, and later for the chantry chaplain.

In 1353/4 at an Inquisition post mortem (see Appendix 4 on page 84) held in Nottingham on 17th February,[11] William de Beckford on the oath of various local gentry, declared certain of his lands and houses in this area, which he wished to give to a chaplain and his successors. This was incumbent upon him, for the founder of a chantry chapel had to provide for its upkeep and for the services of a chaplain who should celebrate the mass there daily and pray for the souls of the founder and his family – in this case, William himself, his father John, mother Felice and his brothers and sisters.

The chapel was duly built and on Sunday, 1st August, 1355 on the Feast of St. Peter ad Vincula, it was dedicated to St. Catherine and John de Beston; a relative of William's was appointed by the Prior and Convent of Lenton. The chapel was situated in the south aisle and traces of it were discovered when the old church was demolished in 1842. On that day, William presented permanent gifts to the chantry, namely a missal, a book of hours, a pair of vestments with towels, a chalice of two marks' weight and a strong box in which to keep the books and ornaments.[12] In addition he gave two oxen worth 24 shillings and three horses worth 30 shillings. The endowment of land contained 34 acres of arable land in Lenton and 45 acres in Beeston, so no doubt the oxen and horses would be a necessity for the profitable cultivation of this land. The chantry was valued at £4 9s 2d.

It is interesting to note that in the twentieth century land on Broadgate and the area covered by the present Peveril Road, Kenilworth Road and Warwick Avenue came into the hands of Mr. F.H. Starling of 'The Oaks', Broadgate. He discovered from the deeds that this land was part of the original endowment of William de Beckford for St. Catherine's chantry. He gave the land back to the church to provide a mission church in that area, but the project was not taken up.[13]

The duties of the chantry priest were given in detail.[14] At mass every day he was to say the Collect 'Dei cui proprum' for the founder and 'inclina' for the souls of his family aforesaid, and to say the Office for the Dead daily except at Eastertide and on double feasts. On Sundays and feasts of the nine lessons, his mass was to be that of the day; on Saturdays of Our Lady, on Wednesdays of St. Catherine. On doubles, if he was in Beeston, he was to help the vicar in reading and singing, taking his hour of mass without prejudice to the vicar. If the chaplain died after the hay and wheat harvest between the Nativity of Our Lady and Christmas, he was to demise a moiety of hay and straw to his successor.

The St. Catherine's chantry chapel was in continuous use from 1355 to 1539 when it was suppressed by Henry VIII at the Dissolution of the monasteries and its endowment was confiscated in Edward VI's reign in 1548. The last of the chantry priests, Alexander Constable, received a pension of £4 0s 3d (see Appendix 5 on page 85) and the original endowment of 45 acres of land in Beeston and 34 acres in Lenton appears to have been sold off and the proceeds went into the royal coffers.[15]

It is clear from the records we have that William de Beckford (or William de Beston as he was later known) was a capable and astute person, well suited to the task allotted to him by his sovereign. Moreover, he was quick to seize opportunities which could lead to his own advancement. He had influential friends here, including William Amyas, a former Mayor of Nottingham and a wealthy wool merchant and shipowner who had many properties in the area and founded the Amyas chantry chapel in St. Mary's Church. Amyas and his wife, Marjorie, both named William as executor in their wills and no doubt he was a beneficiary in both.[16]

William died at Cotgrave in December 1361. It is certain that during his 22 years in this area he became a rich and powerful man and by reason of his work for his sovereign, could command his sovereign's support. By the foundation of the chantry he ensured that he would be remembered for many years to come in Beeston. Had he been living today, there is no doubt he would have risen to fame as a great business man or a successful entrepreneur. As it was, he fulfilled a special need at a critical time, and no other vicar of Beeston, either before or since, has ever been called upon by the sovereign to carry out such an important mission.

Sources (Chapter Four)
[1]Arthur Cossons, Wm. de Beckford, King's Clerk, *Thoroton Society* Vol 39, (1935)
[2]N.R.O. Letters Patent – 15 Edward III
[3]N.R.O. Letters Patent – Cal Pat. Roll 14 Edward III
[4]Calendar Fine Rolls – 1342, p.272
[5]Calendar Fine Rolls – 1349
[6]G.W. Deverill, *History of Beeston Parish Church*, (1927), p.6
[7]Calendar Patent Rolls - 25 Edward III
[8]Arthur Cossons, *William de Beckford - King's Clerk*
[9]J.T. Godfrey, *Transcripts Torre Mss*
[10]Calendar Patent Rolls - 28 Edward III
[11]G.W. Deverill, *History of Beeston Parish Church* (1927), p.13
[12]York Registry, *Transactions of the Thoroton Society*, (1914)
[13]G.W. Deverill, *History of Beeston Parish Church* (1927), p.13
[14]Chantry Cert. Rolls for Nottinghamshire
[15]Arthur Cossons, *Pensioned Chantry Priests*
[16]Alan Cameron, *William Amyas and Community of Nottingham 1308-50*, Thoroton Society (1971), p.77

CHAPTER FIVE

The Later Middle Ages

1. The Village, its layout and its people

Beeston's inhabitants lived mainly along the present Middle Street from Church Street to the City, and along Nether Street. Church Street contained the church, then a small Early English building, the churchyard or God's Acre, the vicarage and a fishpond beyond it. The vicarage would have been small, possibly of wood or wattle and daub, providing accommodation for a celibate priest and his manservant. To the west and north lay the glebe land, to be farmed by the vicar. Nearby, on the site now occupied by the Police Headquarters, was the Grange or Tithe Barn, in which the tithes of corn and hay for Lenton Priory were stored. Below the vicarage and close by the present Crown Inn may have been the village alehouse. This was usually situated near the church, as the church ale was brewed there.

West End and the area surrounding it was probably the land originally belonging to the Danish 'soc' man and this was the estate given to the Argenteon family and eventually around 1200 to Wymondley Priory. On this site may have been the monastic manor house, perhaps near to the present 'Old Manor House'.

At the crossing between Church Street, West End, Middle Street and later Dovecote Lane, stood the village cross. The remains of this cross of medieval origin were discovered embedded in a nearby wall by Mr. Arthur Cossons, our local historian, in 1929. It has now been erected on a plinth and placed outside the Manor School on Church Street.

On the south side of Middle Street near the cross was the site of the Manor House which may have been built for the Peveril family or by the Beauchamps, who were granted the estate by Henry II in 1171. The stone footings and the central cellars of the present Manor House suggest an earlier building which could have been timber framed. Around this house would have been various outbuildings, stables and barns with the Lord's demesne stretching down to the Pasture Dyke in the south and perhaps to the line of the High Road in the north. Manor Lodge was the site of the Manor farmhouse.

24. Remains of Medieval Cross, Church Street

Between the north-east corner of the churchyard and the north-west corner of the Lord's demesne was a small area of common land by the Round Hill. Here was situated a village pinfold - a wooden or stone enclosure in which stray animals were placed by the village pinder. Nearby were the village stocks which by a law of Edward III in 1376 were compulsory in every village. Here wrongdoers were put as a punishment and villagers were able to add further to their discomfort by hurling rotten apples and eggs, etc. at them. The stocks continued in use until about 1840 and the pinfold until about 1890, when the land there was used to erect the first council offices. The approximate site today is that of the 'Argos' store at the north end of the precinct.

From beyond the Manor House and its demesne were the houses of the villagers set in their own crofts near Middle Street and the small cottages of the cottars around the City and Nether Street, which was probably one of the areas of Saxon settlement which continued as the village centre after the arrival of the Normans. This may explain why today it is still called the 'City'. In the larger houses would dwell the tenant farmers and the various village craftsmen. In the cottages would be the smallholders and manor servants. Below Nether Street would be the Pasture Dyke which joined the Tottle Brook in the east and continued to the west via the Robinets. It is possible that a few folk lived over the Pasture Dyke and near to the river, while the miller whose windmill stood high up on the hill towards Bramcote might have had his home there.

Most houses would have been wooden and of the 'cruck' type with wattle and daub in-filling and a thatched or turf roof. The whole would be single-storey and if further room was required, a lean-to shed would be built on the end. Often the walls would be covered with lime plaster to strengthen the clay beneath. Inside the house, the ground space would be divided by wattle hurdles to provide a room for eating and cooking (with a hearth made for the fire), a compartment for sleeping and a further space for the animals. A few apertures were left in the walls to provide light and ventilation, but few houses had glass windows. The single door was made in two parts – the top was opened for light and air, the lower part could be closed to keep the hens and pigs indoors in bad weather.

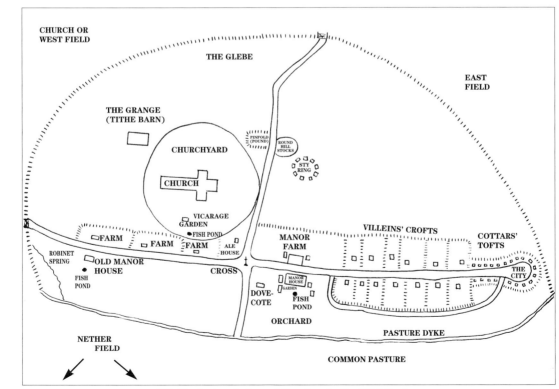

25. Conjectural plan of Beeston in the Middle Ages

Furniture was simple: a wooden table, a few stools and benches, a chest in which to keep clothes, etc., and shelves fixed to the walls. Beds would be straw-filled mattresses placed on the floor at night and rolled up during the day. A wooden bedstead would be a prized possession for poor folk, to be passed on to future generations, as early wills show.

Cooking was done on the open fire in large metal cauldrons made by the village blacksmith, in hanging metal pots suspended by a rod over the fire, or in simple clay pots which could be placed in the hot ashes. Mugs and platters were made of wood or clay and for richer folk, of pewter. Spoons and knives were used but <u>no</u> forks. Their diet was simple – plenty of coarse dark bread home-baked, pottage (a kind of stew with oatmeal), vegetables and a little meat, milk, cheese, butter and eggs with fish from the Trent. Ale was their chief drink with buttermilk and curds and whey for the children. In the summer, apples and pears from their orchards, together with wild berries and nuts would supplement their usual fare. Beehives were to be found in most of the small plots, or tofts, around their homes and the honey from the bees provided the sweetening for their food, and was also used to make mead and metheglin (a spiced form of mead). Herbs which grew wild or were cultivated were used extensively for flavouring stews or pottage and for making homely remedies. Beeston would not have had a doctor during the Middle Ages, so people depended on herbal medicines and those who had the wisdom and skill in using them.

2. Social Life in Beeston in the Middle Ages

In the Middle Ages and even later, life, especially in the villages, was precarious. Almost everyone was dependent on the weather and the villagers' extreme vulnerability to disease meant that mortality rates were high and the expectation of life no more than 40-50 years.

Beeston was a typical Midland village, most of whose inhabitants were peasant farmers, solely dependent on land cultivation for their livelihood. They owned or rented from the Lord of the Manor, strips of land in the great open fields which stretched for many acres around the village. On the west side was Church field, on the east the Tottle Brook field and below the Pasture Dyke was Nether field. These fields were divided into strips 220 yards long and 22 yards wide (hence the standard area of a strip was 4,840 square yards = 1 acre. A villein or villager's usual holding was 30 strips (or acres) – ten in each of the three fields. This holding was sometimes referred to as a 'husbandland', a living, a yardland or a virgate and was as much as could be ploughed by two oxen in a year. Less prosperous villeins would have 15 acres, or a half yardland or a borate. All these holdings were marked out in early times with wooden pegs and passed down from father to son. It is possible to see this strip farming today at Laxton in north Nottinghamshire. Their farming implements were simple, the chief being the fixed mould board plough which produced the typical 'ridge and furrow' still to be seen on ancient fields. The plough would be owned by a group of villeins, who would have provided between them the team of six or eight oxen to draw it. Scythes and sickles were used for reaping and flails and winnowing fans for threshing.

The fields were farmed communally for ploughing, crop rotation, sowing and harvesting, but each family worked its own strips for harrowing, weeding and reaping. It was incumbent upon each villein to erect hurdles of wattle across the ends of his strips to prevent the cattle and other animals from straying from the commons to harm the corn or other growing crops. These hurdles were kept until after the harvest each year, after which time the animals were free to graze there. One field of the three was always left fallow in rotation and this field was used specifically for the grazing of animals. Their dung or manure provided the necessary fertilisers for the next year's crop, and this was considered as valuable as their flesh or hides.

The chief crops grown here were:

Rye or wheat – chiefly the former (hence the Ryelands) and this was used for the making of bread.

Barley – grown for the malt and the making of ale.

Peas, beans, etc. – grown for the pottage.

The rye was sown in the autumn, and the other crops in February or March. All were harvested in August.

The animals were as important as the cultivation of the fields and great care was taken of them, for the families were dependent on them for their livelihood. The oxen worked generally only in the mornings or until 3.00pm, and then were taken to graze on the lush common pasture land by the river. This area was probably fenced off into separate lots with each tenant taking his own share of the hay crop. After 1st August, the meadows were thrown open for the cattle to graze there. Grazing on the common land was jealously regulated and no stranger's beasts were permitted there. Only the commonable beasts, ie oxen, horses and sheep were allowed and a villein who put out more animals than his share could be fined at the Manor Court. Some sheep would be found grazing on the lower pastures and on the wastelands. They were kept above all for their wool and for their manure for the tillage. The ewe's milk could be used for cheese, their skins for parchment, but <u>not</u> their meat, which was tough and stringy!

When meadows, commonland, waste and arable fields were all available for grazing, the animals were reasonably well fed, but never made much fat. However, the scanty food in winter, chiefly dry straw and tree loppings, caused the cattle to be susceptible to murrain and the sheep to scab and foot rot. Consequently, many animals were killed at Michaelmas (25th September) and their carcases were salted down for winter use. Most families kept pigs who scavenged on acorns and beechmast from the woods. Because they fatten quicker than other animals, they were the main source of meat in the winter. The animal hides had many uses: to make leather jerkins, shoes, gloves, harnesses, reins, belts, etc.

In view of the importance of land cultivation, it was necessary for strict rules to be imposed to ensure that each family was able to secure a livelihood. Drainage of the fields was essential and so each man must scour the portion of drains or ditches which ran by his strips.

The possibility of stray animals trespassing on the growing crops was always present. For this reason, an enclosure of wood, wattle or stone was constructed into which stray animals could be placed. This was called a pinfold or pound. Every year at Easter one of the villagers was appointed to take charge of the pinfold and he was called the Pinder. His job was to round up all stray animals, to ascertain their owners and report them to the Manorial Court, who could authorise fines to be paid or punishment exacted before the animals could be released. Sometimes the pinder would be instructed to take an animal from a villager and place it in the pinfold as a surety for a debt. The pinder would generally be excused his duties on the lord's land, and receive help in the cultivation of his own strips during his year of office. A pinder was appointed here until the 1890s, the last one being Mr. William Twiggs who lived on Chapel Street. At that time, Beeston had an Urban District Council and needed a site for its council offices. The pinfold site was chosen as being the only place and anciently belonging to the people of the village, and the first council offices were erected there in 1897.

Full-time employees were such as the miller, the baker, the herdmen, the carpenter, the blacksmith, the weaver, etc. who would be paid in money or in kind, and who could render service to the rest of the villagers at a price. For instance, it was obligatory for all to have their corn ground into flour by the miller. Water mills had been used for this, but by the thirteenth century windmills had become more important. We believe Beeston's windmill may have been situated in the north-west corner of the Church Field, near the top of Bramcote Road and the footpath through the Golf links.

Unfree men and women could be servants doing menial tasks in the manor house or farm, and living in poor accommodation there; or those occupying small wooden cottages in the village and known as 'cottars'. This latter group were considered as slaves and could be bought and sold as chattels. It was even possible for villeins to be sold or given away when their land holding passed to a new owner.[1] In 1241 John and Richard de Beauchamp (the Lords of the Manor) gave two borates of land (approximately 30 acres) to Lenton Priory together with Jordan, son of Yvo, who was a tenant there, with his family and chattels.

About the same time, in 1240, John, son of Robert, a bondman living at the 'Corner in Bestune' was sold by Sybil de Beauchamp together with his children and chattels to Henry de Matloc for half a mark (6s 8d).[2] About ten years afterwards Sybil's son Henry de Puterel gave a release to Roger, son of Ralph de Beston, of John and all his offspring and chattels. "*For this demission and release Roger has paid him 28/- beforehand. Henry and his heirs shall warrant John with all his offspring and chattels to Roger as a freeman and quit of all bondage service.*" This was most unusual to sell a bondman without a landholding, but in this instance the eventual result was good, in that John and his heirs were now declared as freemen, thanks to the generosity of John's relative, Roger de Beston.

By the fourteenth century and perhaps before this, it was not always possible for all to be employed on the manor lands or on the family holdings, so some men were compelled to join the stream of immigrants to Nottingham and other towns, where they might earn a living as country craftsmen or textile and leather workers. This may explain the position of those men surnamed 'de Beston' who are to be found in Nottingham during the thirteenth and fourteenth centuries.

Law and Order and Obligations

Apart from the laws of the land, the villagers would have to conform to local regulations laid down by the Lord of the Manor and the Honour of the Peveril Court (see Chapter 3). From early times, the men and boys over 12 were placed in groups of ten or twelve, all of whom were mutually responsible for the good behaviour of each other. This was called a "Frankpledge". Twice a year, the Sheriff (or Shire Reeve) visited each Hundred or Wapentake Court to view the Frankpledge and ensure that no man was living in a village or hamlet outside the Frankpledge.[3] The Lord of the Manor was exempt, as were his servants, as he was deemed to be responsible for their good behaviour. Freemen and soc men too, were not required to join a Frankpledge.

Serious crimes such as murder came under the Assize Court held in Nottingham each quarter. Sometimes the murderer fled the village before he could be apprehended and became an outlaw. Killing of the King's deer in Sherwood Forest or in the royal parks was punishable by death and some of these offenders, like Robin Hood, escaped to the forest and became outlaws. Crimes involving the misuse of land and the failure to scour ditches or repair bridges came under the Honour of Peveril Court. We have evidence, from the Court Rolls of Henry VI's time, of misdemeanours of certain Beeston men which will be referred to in a later chapter.

Purely local Beeston offences such as permitting cattle to stray into the corn fields were dealt with by the Manorial Court. Unfortunately, these Manorial records have not been found, but the University Library has a Manorial Court roll of 1296 for the neighbouring village of Toton which tells of those who transgressed in this way. Most were fined 3d or 4d for each offence. This was a large amount in those days, for most unskilled labourers earned only 1d or 1d per day. It is interesting and pleasing to learn from the Toton Roll that a woman offender was amerced or excused, owing to her poverty.

Apart from the local and national laws, there were serious obligations incumbent upon the villagers by the Lord of the Manor or his representative in Beeston. All had to use the Lord's mill, high up on Church North Field, for the grinding of their corn and his brewery for the brewing of ale. No animals, land or grain could be sold without the Lord's permission. When a villein died, the Lord could claim as Heriot his best beast and when the succession to the property was approved by the Manor Court, his successor had to pay an entry fine.

The marriage of a villein's daughter required payment of a fine called the Merchet to the Lord. A villein could neither educate his son nor send him to learn a craft or even enter him into the Church without permission. It was forbidden for any to leave or live away from Beeston. However, as Nottingham became more important in the fourteenth and fifteenth centuries, some Beeston men managed to escape there and if they could live there for a year and a day, they were considered as freemen. This may explain the various Beeston men who are mentioned in Nottingham in the fourteenth century and onwards, such as Gilbert de Beeston who had a building in the Saturday Market in 1300, John de Beeston in 1354 who was a tanner, William de Beeston in 1375, a bailiff, and Roger de Beeston in 1379 who was a sole decannery (or constable) in Barker Gate.

Taxation, then as now, loomed large as the King demanded more from his subjects to cover his additional expenditure. Knights such as the successive members of the Beauchamp family who were Lords of the Manor here, were required to pay fees of £2. It is just possible that the knights might pay this themselves, but it is certain that the inevitable extra taxes levied would fall upon the men of Beeston.

In 1169 Henry II's daughter was married and the Sheriff of Nottingham demanded the sum of 13s 4d from each village towards the wedding expenses. In 1199 the Lord of the Manor here was ordered to pay £14 towards King John's coronation and we may be sure that this was levied on the villagers, who would, if they knew, be very angry to learn that on both occasions the village of Arnold was only required to pay half these amounts. King John himself was to incur the wrath of his subjects for he imposed illegal taxes ten times during his reign and often at double the previous amount. It was, in fact, the levying of these illegal and exorbitant taxes which was one of the causes of the great confrontation between the barons and John which culminated in the Magna Carta of 1215.

In the fourteenth century the wars between England and France (the Hundred Years' War) caused additional demands on the Crown revenue. Parliament, which had been officially founded in 1265, gave permission for subsidies to be granted to the Crown in the form of taxes on the wealth of the laity. In 1316 a list was made of all towns, villages, etc (Nomine Villarieim) in which Beeston was listed as a 'whole Vill' for taxation purposes. Thus the village people were included in these lay subsidies and were taxed on their movable goods, that is crops and stock, other than land. Assessment was done by two chief taxers for each county and four sub-taxers for each taxation unit. These went from house to house in the village, usually at Michaelmas, valuing the moveable goods and recording the information. Taxation varied each year from $1/9$ to $1/20$ of the valuation according to the need. Tax payments were summarised and written on an indented roll and the assessment was made of the whole of the community, not on individuals.

In 1334 Beeston's lay subsidy tax was £5 5s 5d, the largest amount in the Broxtowe division. In 1348 Roger de Beauchamp as Lord of the Manor was required to pay an additional £2 towards the Knighting of the Black Prince, after his victory at the Battle of Crecy.

Markets and Fairs
These were of great importance in the Middle Ages. For the inhabitants of Beeston they would give them the opportunity to sell their surplus produce and stock and to buy in scarce commodities. From the time of Henry I (c1155) Nottingham had been granted the right to hold a market on Fridays and Saturdays and it was to this market just three miles away that the Beeston folk would generally go.[4] Tolls and taxes had to be paid for the privilege of entering Nottingham on market days, particularly if one was intending to sell. There is some evidence that Beeston was exempt from certain taxes because it had been a royal estate. The highlights of the year would be the great fairs which could last from eight to fifteen days.

Nottingham's Michaelmas Fair lasted from 21st September to 9th October, and, later to be called the famous Goose Fair, was especially popular. A second fair was granted and this was held about the Feast of King Edmund the Martyr and lasted fifteen days. About 1163 Henry II granted the right to hold a fair at Lenton Priory. This was held around Martinmas (11th November) and it developed into one of the largest and most important in the country.[5] Traders would come from as far away as London and elsewhere to sell their goods – luxury items such as fine woven cloth from Flanders and exotic fruits and spices from the East. The great attraction of these fairs would be the merrymaking and the various forms of entertainment such as juggling and bear baiting, which the Beeston folk and many others would enjoy to the full.

3. People of the Village
Apart from the Lords of the Manor and the Vicars (which are covered elsewhere in the text) we know little of the other inhabitants except for those who are mentioned from time to time in various legal documents. During the fourteenth century, Maud Roter, Hugh Maister, Galfrid Poutrell and Robert Daft rented or owned land here. The Daft family appear consistently in records up to the 1900s. William de Beckford appears in a chantry bequest. Richard Willoughby, who owned land in Sutton Passeys and Wollaton, had a grant of free warren here in 1354 which seems to have continued with the Willoughby family for centuries.

Most names recorded are of wrongdoers. Fine Rolls of 1280 mention the case of two brothers, John and Simon de Beeston, who had entered the town of Nottingham unlawfully and trespassed there. For this they were fined, imprisoned and forbidden to enter the town for a year. Upon them giving surety for good behaviour, the justices ordered them to be given free entry to the town. Similar instructions were also given to Richard Lambok, Richard Curzon, Adam Daft and Adam Fleming, who probably came from Beeston.

In 1330 the Prior of Lenton made a charge against certain Beeston men who had broken into his house, taken goods and assaulted his servants.[6] We do not know the outcome of this charge. In 1353, at the Pleas of Court held at Beeston, the Prior of Lenton, some of his monks and others were accused of the death of Nicholas de Wollaton. Among the accused were John Bailok and Richard Gijon of Beeston. However the justices, Willoughby and Trussebot, tried the case and the jury found them not guilty and they were given restitution of their possessions.[7]

In 1389 Henry Hazard was pardoned out of regard for Good Friday of his outlawry for the death of Katherine, the wife of William Wright of Beeston, who was killed in the fields of Sallowe.[8]

The Court of Peverel in Henry VI's reign mentioned a number of Beeston residents who were fined for illegal brewing and selling the ale against the assize.[9] These were Gervase Bampton, Peter Bates, Henry Smith, William Smith, William Claygate, Thomas Attenborough, Robert de Wilford, Richard Rhodes, William Pate, Hugh Rhodes, Robert and Ralph Bates, Peter Bates jnr, Thomas Bates and Robert Clark. This seems to have been mainly offences of the Bates, Smith and Rhodes families. Each was fined 2d – a normal labourer's daily wage was 1d.

Another case was of John Taylor who attacked Richard Bates and drew blood, while Richard retaliated by drawing blood on John. Both received similar fines, as did John Farthing for drawing blood on Robin Coke of Bramcote, and this against the King's Peace. One lady is mentioned – Mabel Warner, who was fined 4d for non-payment of rent on her shop.

In a further Court Roll, Henry Clark, Ralph Bates, Hugh Baker and William Sage are named as sureties in the view of Frankpledge for the following offenders: John Manchester, Robert Hey, Roger Willerby, Thomas Rawlins, Peter Bates, John Baker, William Claygate, Thomas Wynhurst, William Daft, Hugh Rhodes, John Bates, William Godfrey, Roger Attenborough and others who brewed illegally and sold against the assize.[10]

The Bampton family appears to be prominent in the fifteenth and sixteenth centuries in the village. In 1430 Gervase Bampton was noted as a juror in a prominent lawsuit between Sir John Bertram and Sir Ralph Cromwell.[11] In 1482 John Bampton was chosen to represent the Wapentake of Broxtowe. He, with others, and by a local agreement from the County Wapentakes, were obliged to arrange for the repair of the Leen bridge. As this work was not carried out, he and the others were distrained (ie deprived of their property).[12] In 1503/4 another Gervase Bampton of Beeston was taxed 29s 6d for the land he owned near the Hen Cross in Nottingham. This was a comparatively small amount, the large landowners there paid much more!

The surname Beeston or de Beeston occurs here and in Nottingham. In 1438 Thomas and Robert Beeston, sons of the late Richard Beeston of Beeston, granted lands here to Nicholas Willoughby, Henry and William Warner, together with other rents and services. This deed was witnessed by John Manchester, who may be the same John Manchester who was mentioned in the Peverel Court Roll.

4. The Black Death 1348-9

This terrible catastrophe, the rapid spread of the bubonic plague, brought by way of the trade routes from the East, began in England in 1348 in the south. The lethal nature of the disease, characterised by the black spots on the skin, caused alarm and dread throughout the country. The Archbishop of York ordered that special prayers were to be said each Wednesday and Friday and penitential processions and masses for 'pro mortalitate' were prescribed in the diocese of Southwell in November 1348. In March 1349 the plague probably reached our area and was at its height from May to July. In Newark in May a new cemetery had to be consecrated to accommodate the bodies of the victims. In Nottingham the normal collection of river tolls and pontage duties had to be neglected because of the plague. The clergy of the area were particularly affected – over 35% of those in the Nottingham deanery died that year, including Astorgius, the Prior of Lenton.

Although we have no figures for the deaths in Beeston, it is possible that at least 30% of the inhabitants died from the disease. In 1361/2 the plague struck again and this time it was the young people who had not built up an immunity to the plague who were the chief victims. Finally, in 1369 there was a further, but less severe outbreak. Thus, before the end of the century the population in the village was considerably reduced. The results of this sudden decline was especially devastating in such a small village as Beeston. The Lord of the Manor had fewer servants and craftsmen to work on his land and property, and these were discontented by the burden of additional duties and rightly demanded higher wages. In the south, this was to culminate in the Peasants' Revolt under Wat Tyler.

The villagers, who were obliged to help on the manor lands at busy times such as harvest and ploughing, were now fewer in number. In addition, the deaths of whole families, a not uncommon experience, meant that their holdings reverted to the Lord of the Manor, thus making his estate even larger and duties greater. Some peasants who had acquired or earned a little wealth took advantage of this situation to rent additional land from the Lord of the Manor and become yeoman farmers. This encouraged the growth of individual enterprise, which was to become apparent in succeeding centuries. It is possible that the rise in prosperity of such families as the Levis, the Laceys, the Dafts and the Smalleys may have begun then. There was too a reservoir of landless men who were willing to take up villein status in return for land and this gave the Lord additional profits from his new holdings.

It was abundantly clear that in future there would be fewer workers on the land and changes must be made in its use. Wise owners decided to turn over some of their acreage to sheep-rearing instead of arable farming, for this required fewer men. This must have happened in Beeston, for in 1479 Edmund Harroppe is reported to have received by bequest 20 sheep, which assumes that the beneficiary had sufficient ground to graze them.

It is just possible that around this time part of one of the great open fields may have been enclosed by one or a group of villagers to enable them to graze more sheep. This may have been the Horse Doles Closes which are mentioned as early as 1325 as being held in severalty, ie by a group of villagers. We have evidence too of villagers becoming tenants of farms, leasing their stock and implements from the Lord and thus gaining a certain independence from feudal dues.[13]

Sources (Chapter Five)
[1]Robert Mellors, *In and About Nottinghamshire*, p.11
[2]Wollaton Hall M.S.S., pp.62-3
[3]Steaton, *English Society in the Early Middle Ages*
[4]G. Trease, *Biography of Nottingham*, p.36
[5]Godfrey, *History of Lenton*
[6]Patent Rolls 1354
[7]Pleas Patent Rolls 1354
[8]Patent Rolls 1389
[9]Court of Peverel 1428
[10]ibid
[11]Robert Mellors, *In and About Nottinghamshire*
[12]ibid
[13]A.C. Wood, *History of Nottinghamshire*, p.88-90

CHAPTER SIX

Beeston under the Tudors 1485-1603

Henry VII (1485-1509) had to contend with a rising by the army of the pretender Lambert Simnel in 1487 which culminated in the Battle of Stoke Field at East Stoke on the A46. Local knights and their retainers were ordered to support the King. Amongst them was Sir John Babington, who owned land here and in Chilwell, so it is possible that local men would have been recruited into the King's army. The Muster Array of 1539 showed that Beeston had 15 able-bodied men eligible to bear arms.

In 1488 Henry renewed a privilege to Beeston granted originally by Richard II of exemption of tolls, stallage and chiminage. Stallage related to the liberty to erect a stall at a market or fair. This would give Beeston tenants the right to erect such a stall at the Nottingham markets and at Lenton Fair and the Goose Fair. Chiminage was the toll paid to the forest ranger for the liberty of passage through the forest or a tax paid by wayfarers travelling along roads from place to place.

1. Changes in the Manorial Rights

The Beauchamp family who had held the larger estate here since 1171 appeared to have died out in the male line from the late fourteenth century. It seemed that by this time, much of this land had passed into the hands of Sir John Babington, the Lord of the Manor of Chilwell. No doubt he would take a greater interest in the village than the previous owners, who were absentee landlords, relying on a resident steward or bailiff to administer the estate. In 1501, however, Sir John died – the last of the male line – and his estates passed to one of his nieces, Elena Delves. On her marriage in 1504 to Sir Robert Sheffield, she brought the Manor of Beeston and other estates as her dowry. Thoroton (in his History of Nottinghamshire) mentions that Sir Robert sold off some Beeston lands to William Smalley, Thomas Charlton and other freeholders.

However, in 1523, Sir Robert acknowledged that properties here were the right of Sir John Hussey of Sleaford, as Lord of the Manor. Unfortunately, in 1536 Sir John was executed for his complicity in the 'Pilgrimage of Grace', a movement against the Act of Supremacy. Presumably his estates and manorial rights here returned to the Crown, where they remained until Elizabethan times.

The Wymondley Priory lands here continued as before until Henry VIII's time. Already some land in the village was in the hands of freeholders, such as the Smalley and Levis families.

2. Religious Developments

The Rebuilding of the Church

This took place during the early years of the sixteenth century. The walls of the chancel, the image niche, the Piscina and the Sedilia of the fourteenth century church were incorporated into the new building of Perpendicular style. It consisted of a nave and chancel with a south

26. Beeston Church, prior to 1841

aisle which would form the chantry chapel of St. Katherine. Beyond this, a tower was erected which contained three bells and a clock. Adjoining this was a porch providing entry into the nave. The building could accommodate 270 people. It is depicted in the South Nottinghamshire tapestry (made in the early 1600s) now in the Costume Museum in Nottingham, and a painting of the church as it appeared before 1841 can still be seen in the Vicar's Vestry. The Vicarage with its fourteenth century timbers was not rebuilt until 1860.

Henry VIII (1509-47) instigated great changes everywhere, especially when he became Supreme Head of the Church. Just prior to this, in 1535, he had ordered a Valuation of all ecclesiastical properties (*Valor Ecclesiasticus*). Beeston is listed and full details are given of the tithes to be exacted and the value of the benefice is given as £4 15s 0d. The chantry chapel is mentioned with the value of the priest's appointment as £4 9s 2d. In view of the greater work to be done by the vicar, there is no wonder that he must have been envious of the chantry priest!

The Dissolution of the Monasteries 1537-9

In 1537, Henry, through Parliament, ordered the dissolution of the smaller monasteries and priories. This included Wymondley Priory and as a result, the monastic manor here, held by the Priory since about 1200, was granted to James Needham (gent) for an annual rental of 69s 4d. Subsequently, he sold it to William Bolles and eventually the manor returned to the Crown, possibly due to distraint. In 1599, Elizabeth granted it to Benjamin Harris and Robert Morgan at a rental of £9.

In 1539, the larger monasteries were dissolved and this included Lenton Priory, to which Beeston had been appropriated from about 1230, so the consequences of this event were more far-reaching. The advowson – the right to present a vicar – now passed to Henry VIII and his successors until 1603, apart from a short spell in 1558-62 when it was granted to the Archbishop of York. The various tithes were granted, presumably for a rental, to certain gentlemen. In 1539 William Fitzwilliam was granted the hay tithes and in 1540 Edmund Molyneux, sergeant at law, had a grant of lease of 21 years of all tithes of corn belonging to the vicarage and a parcel of land here in which a grange (tithe barn) was formerly situated. For this he paid £9 for the tithes and 4d for the land, which must have been very small!

Suppression of the Chantries 1547-8

This included our St. Katherine's Chantry founded by William de Beckford in 1355 and taken over by the Crown in 1539. Its endowment was suppressed in 1547/8. The chantry priest at that time, Alexander Constable, then aged 40, was later (in 1555) granted a pension of £4 0s 3d. The endowment, valued at £4 9s 2d annually, was 45 acres of land in Beeston and 34 acres in Lenton, with houses at both places.

In 1549 Michael Stanhope was granted a rood of land in Beeston, which had provided for a lamp at the altar, probably at the chantry chapel.

The English Bible

Henry VIII ordered Miles Coverdale to make a new translation of the Bible in English. This was published in 1535 and in 1538 all clergy were ordered to set up a copy of this Bible in their churches and to encourage their parishioners to read it. No doubt this was done in Beeston, but sadly neither this nor its lectern have survived.

Edward VI (1547-53) continued to support the Protestant religion. In 1547/9 an Inventory of Church Plate and Vestments was ordered for each parish. From this we learn that Beeston possessed:

    3 bells in steeple
    2 vestments of chargeable silk (shot silk)
    1 vestment of fustian
    2 cowls of chargeable silk
    2 altar cloths
    1 chalice of silver
    2 cruets
    1 cross of wood covered with brass
    1 handbell (possibly for ringing at the sanctus)
    1 perpetual light before the altar

(The provision of the light was from land rented by the church wardens and cows pastured upon it.)

The chantry chapel plate – crucifix and ornaments – were valued at 3s 9d in 1547 (a previous valuation in 1535 was 5s 6d, which suggests that some articles were hidden or sold!).

The reign of **Mary Tudor** (1553-58) saw the return of the Roman Catholic religion and the persecution of many Protestants, including Archbishop Cranmer, Bishops Ridley and Latimer with over 300 lay folk who were burnt at the stake.

The Vicar of Beeston, John Mottram, resigned his living in 1557, possibly through fear of persecution. This gave Mary the opportunity to appoint a Roman Catholic, Nicholas Holmes, to the benefice.

The reign of **Elizabeth I** (1558-1603) saw a return to the Protestant religion with the use of the English Bible and Prayer Book. Fines were imposed on those who absented themselves from church services. It seems likely that Nicholas Holmes resigned his living on Elizabeth's accession and the Archbishop of York appointed John Fisher to succeed him. With hindsight, this must be considered an unsatisfactory appointment, for he was often brought before the Archdeacon's Court. His chief offences were his neglect of the vicarage and church fabric, failing to preach the required two sermons per quarter, and finally reading a slanderous libel in the church service, which caused grave disquiet to the parishioners. So serious were his misdemeanours that it was decided to sequestrate the vicarage, but he died in 1592 before this could be done. He was succeeded by William Jeffreis, who will be remembered for the courageous part he played in the great tragedy which befell the village soon after this.

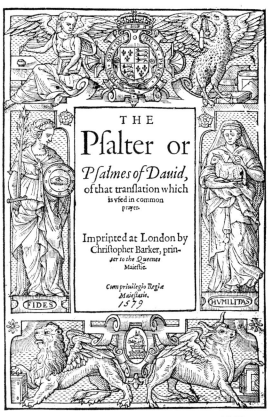

27. Frontispiece of a Breeches Bible, 1579

3. The Strey Family: Lords of the Manor of Beeston c1560-1797

From 1536 to c1560, Beeston was in the hands of the Crown. Elizabeth was in need of money and prepared to grant the privilege of the Lord of the Manor to whoever could pay for it.

The Strey family who gained it came originally from Greasley, and Nicholas Strey was the first to become chief landowner in the village. He was also granted the right to collect the hay tithes formerly paid to Lenton Priory. The field where the hay was stacked was just south of the Manor house (which now houses the Venn Court complex). It is quite likely that the Manor House in which he and his family lived for many years was a timber-framed house, and the present stone steadings could have been from this earlier house.

Nicholas and his son (also called Nicholas) seem to have thought highly of themselves and wished others to do so. Thoroton, the County historian, called them 'petty squires' but they considered themselves as gentry. They displayed armorial bearings (sable, on a chevron engraved *argent*, between three lions' heads erased *or*; as many cinquefoils *gules*) without obtaining permission from Norroy King of Arms. In 1614 Nicholas II put in a

28. Arms of the Strey Family

claim to be called 'gentleman' but this was refused. At the Herald's Visitation that same year, he disclaimed that he had displayed armorial bearings, but nevertheless the family continued to do so!

However, the will of Nicholas I (20th February, 1604) shows that as well as bequests to family and servants, he was mindful of the needs of the people of the village, and he gave 5 shillings to provide stone for the making of bridges and stepping stones in the Nether Field. The field adjoined the Pasture Dyke whose flooding would make wooden bridges unsafe.

Very little is known of the later Streys apart from their wills and mentions in legal matters. John Strey (1666-96) was treasurer for the south of the county and it seems likely that the present frontage of the Manor House was built during his time. It has been dated as c1675 by the Nottingham Building Preservation Trust. Nicholas Strey IV probably added the east wing with its characteristic Dutch gable about 1700-25. Nicholas Strey V (1746-85) appealed against the Poor Rate Assessment and refused to pay his church assessment.

Richard Strey (1785-97), the last Lord of the Manor, was formerly a lawyer in Nottingham. He was remembered by old inhabitants as 'an easy going personage of middle height, ordinarily dressed in a brown coat and fond of going out coursing on his great pony'.[1]

The last of the direct line of the Streys was Richard's sister, Dorothy, who continued to live at the Manor House until 1802. She was reputed to be short tempered and penurious to a degree. Her costume was quaint, and she always wore a mob cap. Poor children of the village would remember the family's custom of distributing Hot Cross Buns at the door of the Manor House on Good Friday.

29. Beeston Manor House

By the twentieth century there had been some deterioration of the Manor house structure and on the advice of the Nottingham Building Preservation Trust the chimney tops were rebuilt, some re-tiling was done, iron ties were erected in the garrets of the main range and a damp course was inserted. Above all, the nineteenth century rough cast rendering was removed to reveal the original brickwork and openings. The restoration work was carried out in 1981 with generous aid from the Trust and the European Heritage Fund, for which we are most grateful.

4. The Plague in Beeston 1593-4

From the time when the Black Death reached England in 1348 and spread throughout the land, the plague's recurrence was an ever-present anxiety. It was soon evident that there were two main types – ***the pneumonic*** which attacked the lungs and was quickly spread by the victim's cough; this was probably the type which caused the Black Death; and ***the bubonic*** type, which seemed milder in comparison, but was most horrible in reality. It produced monstrous swellings of the lymphatic glands and terrible sickness. This type was spread by fleas found in the bodies of black rats which inhabited many of the dirty and insanitary houses of that time.

Plague sufferers were offered various remedies – one recipe suggested 2lb figs, two handfuls of rue with 60 blanched walnuts beaten small – a tedious task! If this did not work, the patients could try roasted onions filled with treacle and pepper which may have been a more suitable remedy for the poor folk of that time. Some preachers had their own medicines, such as "take a pound of good hard penance and wash it well with the water of your eyes"!

In May 1593, a mysterious illness attacked Beeston and it is almost certain that this was the dreaded bubonic plague. The first victim may have died on 17 May, but by the end of June, 14 burials had been recorded. Normally there were only seven or eight per year. The Parish Register shows that of these 14 burials, seven were from the Reckless family – the father John, his wife Joan, and their five children. By the end of July, the number of burials that month had dropped to eight and the villagers may have assumed that the disease was on the wane. However, by August, the number had risen to ten, with a further 16 added in September, by which time the disease had reached epidemic proportions, with 34 burials in October, 33 in November and another 12 in the first half of December. On many days, there were two or three burials and on one day, 5th November, there were five! This must have presented problems for the Vicar, Rev. William Jefferies and the grave-digger. Eventually, the majority of bodies were buried in a communal grave situated at the east end of the churchyard, and known as the Plague Pit. In January 1594, burials declined to five with a further three in March, when the disease seems to have ended. In all, 138 burials were recorded during the ten months of the epidemic of which 86 took place during the three months between 21st September and 13th December, 1593.[2] (See Appendix 6 on page 85).

Although it is impossible at this distance of time to know from which parts of the village the disease originated, it is probable that the low-lying swampy area around the Pasture Dyke and Nether Field, where the small timbered houses of the villagers were clustered, provided ideal conditions for the flea-ridden black rats. Among the many names of victims it is interesting that there were none from the Strey family who had built their stone manor house on the higher ground near the church. That family was indeed most fortunate for scarcely any other family was unaffected by the pestilence.

35 families lost at least two members of their immediate family and some many more. Apart from the Reckless family (mentioned earlier), seven members of the Browne and James families, five members of the Waplington, Levis and Shrigley families and four members of the Jellibrand, Olyn and Gaudie families perished.

If we assume the population prior to the outbreak to have been between 300 and 350, it will be seen that the proportion of deaths – over 40% – exceeds that of the Black Death and the famous London Plague of 1665. Extensive research by the late Arthur Cossons into the wills of some Beeston inhabitants of this time have revealed some interesting details of the occupations and possessions of two of the plague victims.[3]

The first to be mentioned is one Thomas Arnold – a yeoman farmer – who made his will on 10th October. From his bequests: a store of rye, but no mention of barley or wheat, it may be that he farmed land in the Ryelands area (below the Nether Field and bordering the Trent) where the marshy land would be particularly unhealthy. He seems to have been a man of some means and generous; leaving a quarter of rye to be distributed to the poor of the parish, sixpences and shillings to his godchildren, nephews and nieces and the cancelling of a debt to a relative. His brother was to have his best hat, a pair of green cloth (breeches), a pair of blue stockings and his sword; his brother-in-law his best doublet and coat. The rest of his clothing was for a servant and all his other goods and chattels for his wife.

Then follows a phrase which shows us that Thomas Arnold realised that he was dying of plague and that his wife may soon be a victim, for he says "But of this sickness" and then he gives a fresh disposition of the goods that would have been his widow's. His cattle and sheep, his four hives of bees, his stock of rye, his bedstead with the cupboard, the (linen) press, the framed table and his Bible were to go to various friends, relations and farm servants. His wife's sister was left all his wife's best apparel, her linen and her bedding. Mary Clarke was to have his wife's best hat, her old gown and her petticoat. William Bunting and Henry Hopkinson were left twenty shillings each in money because, he said 'I understand they dare not meddle with my goods' – a suggestion of the realisation that the disease could be spread through contact with a victim's goods or clothes.

Thomas Arnold died early in November and was buried on 6th November. His wife appears to have survived, but their daughter Joanna was an early victim, which may explain the lack of reference to her in his will.

The second will was that of Matthew Baylie, a weaver, who made his will on 11th October – the day after Thomas Arnold, probably dictating it to the Vicar. His wife, Ann and son, Christopher, had already fallen victims to the plague and had died four days earlier, so he left to his friends and relatives his wife's best frock, her best petticoat and half her linen – except the sheets. His mother-in-law was to have her black russet coat with a damask overbody. Two of his fellow villagers were to have his hat, his doublet, his best overstockings and his leather breeches. The remainder of his wife's linen, except the sheets, her best smock, her old petticoat, her best hose and her shoes, were left to a woman servant. The poignant phrase _except the sheets' may suggest again that the used sheets might spread the contagion. Alas, Matthew himself died the following day.

The effects of the plague on such a small community must have been tremendous. With whole families wiped out, the cultivation of their arable strips in the three great open fields would be halted, houses and barns would be left derelict and livestock untended. Even where only one or two members of a family died, extra burdens of agricultural work would be placed on the survivors. Village crafts would suffer too, though with a depleted population it is possible that this may not have been too serious except for specialist crafts. The problem of land cultivation under these new conditions was overwhelming. Thus it is easy to see that the rearing of sheep in preference to arable farming would be considered a better proposition, requiring fewer workers to care for the animals and producing greater profits through the sale of livestock and the wool.

It is highly probable that areas of land in the Nether Field – which may have been most seriously affected by the deaths of their tenants – was turned over to sheep rearing and specially enclosed for this purpose. This may have been done by the two largest landowners, namely the Vicar and the lord of the manor, Nicholas Strey, who would stand to gain most by such conversion.

The story of this village tragedy can only be scanty, culled as it is from the burials recorded with meticulous care in the Parish Registers by the Vicar, Rev. William Jefferies, at the time of the pestilence. Alas, we have no record of the deeds of heroism, of voluntary separations from the surrounding villages or of similar outbreaks nearby. It is good to know that in spite of the toll of this dread disease, some of the family names recorded – the Waplingtons, Smalleys, Attenboroughs and Willimotts – are still to be found in Beeston today.

Sources (Chapter Six)
[1] J.T. Oldrini, *Gleanings* N.R.O.
[2]Parish Registers 1558-1605
[3]Arthur Cossons, 'The Plague Strikes', *Nottinghamshire Countryside* Vol 20

CHAPTER SEVEN

17th and 18th Century Developments

1. Early Enclosures

By this time the village was showing signs of independence. There were many freeholders such as the Levis, Kirkby and Smalley families farming their own lands and only a few villagers were involved with manorial rights. Nottingham was growing and needing more meat and dairy produce for its wealthy gentry and craftsmen, and this could be obtained from the animals on Beeston's grasslands.

About 1610, at the instigation of the vicar, Walter Kynnersley, ably supported by Nicholas Strey, the Lord of the Manor and the farmers, it was agreed that some parts of the village's fields be converted to grassland without Parliamentary sanction. As a result, Nicholas Strey, who had the rights of the hay tithes, stood to gain considerably, and declared that these tithes were the 'richest flower in his garden'. The vicar too, as receiver of the tithes of calves, lambs, milk and wool could also echo this sentiment.

The loser was the Earl of Devonshire, the owner of the corn tithes. For a time some freeholders continued to pay these tithes, even though they were now producing hay, but the Earl was being deprived of a large part of his dues. This had been valued originally at £42 yearly as against hay tithes of £8 yearly. Consequently, in 1662/3 the Earl felt obliged to bring a lawsuit against a number of Beeston farmers for the non-payment of composition in lieu of tithes. The farmers concerned were: Thomas Charlton (of Chilwell Hall), Nicholas Strey, Gilbert West, Clement Bingham, Robert Lacey, Richard and Robert Topley, Richard Reckless, Edward and Richard Levis, Thomas Constable, Leonard Bostocke, Christopher Levis, Robert Kirkby and Thomas James. As a result, a commissioner was sent here to interview and take statements from local witnesses and a good deal of evidence was found of enclosures even before 1610 as well as subsequently. The result of the lawsuit is unknown.

It is possible that as early as 1086 (the time of the Domesday Survey) the Horse Doles Closes (the two southerly projections into the neighbouring parish of Lenton: see fig. 30) were enclosed and held in severalty. By the end of the sixteenth century at least three other closes are mentioned: *Robinet Close* is in the will of John Bampton in 1586. This, being very near the houses and crofts, may never have been part of the open field. *Hassock Close* is included in the will of John Dale in 1589 but Christopher Levis (presumably one of the enclosurers) in his will of 1616 gives evidence that part of the Hassocks was still open. *Browne Close* is mentioned in the will of Edward Raven, a weaver, in 1600. This may have been a croft in or near Station Road, which was formerly called Brown Lane. Christopher Turpin's will of 1603 mentions a close commonly called 'Stone House', which may have been the *'Barn Close'* of the 1809 Tithe Award.

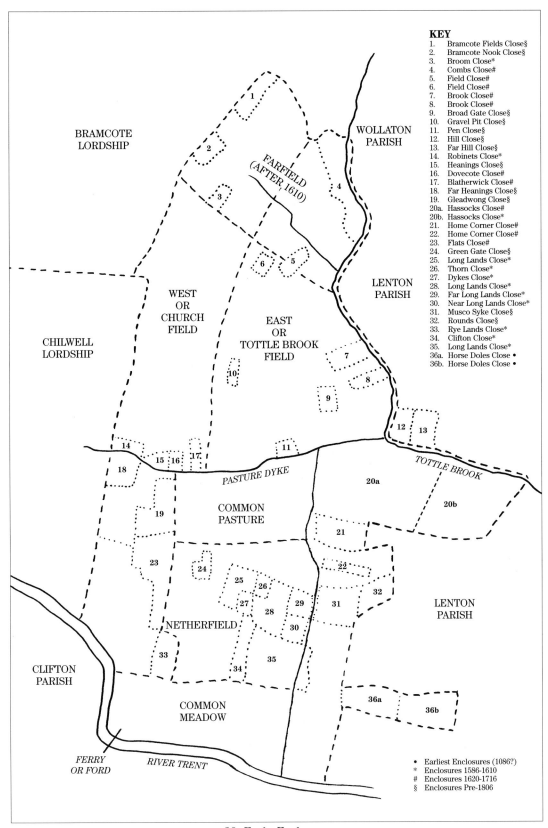

KEY

1. Bramcote Fields Close§
2. Bramcote Nook Close§
3. Broom Close*
4. Combs Close#
5. Field Close#
6. Field Close#
7. Brook Close#
8. Brook Close#
9. Broad Gate Close§
10. Gravel Pit Close§
11. Pen Close§
12. Hill Close§
13. Far Hill Close§
14. Robinets Close*
15. Heanings Close§
16. Dovecote Close#
17. Blatherwick Close#
18. Far Heanings Close§
19. Gleadwong Close§
20a. Hassocks Close#
20b. Hassocks Close*
21. Home Corner Close#
22. Home Corner Close#
23. Flats Close#
24. Green Gate Close§
25. Long Lands Close*
26. Thorn Close*
27. Dykes Close*
28. Long Lands Close*
29. Far Long Lands Close*
30. Near Long Lands Close*
31. Musco Syke Close§
32. Rounds Close§
33. Rye Lands Close*
34. Clifton Close*
35. Long Lands Close*
36a. Horse Doles Close •
36b. Horse Doles Close •

BRAMCOTE
LORDSHIP

WOLLATON
PARISH

FARFIELD
(AFTER, 1610)

LENTON
PARISH

WEST
OR
CHURCH
FIELD

CHILWELL
LORDSHIP

EAST
OR
TOTTLE BROOK
FIELD

PASTURE DYKE

TOTTLE BROOK

COMMON
PASTURE

LENTON
PARISH

NETHERFIELD

CLIFTON
PARISH

COMMON
MEADOW

FERRY
OR FORD

RIVER TRENT

• Earliest Enclosures (1086?)
* Enclosures 1586-1610
# Enclosures 1620-1716
§ Enclosures Pre-1806

30. Early Enclosures

43

The main enclosure, and the largest, was the Nether Field, which seems to have been altered about 1610 and the villagers' pasture rights there were discontinued. The field was one of the original three fields dating from Saxon times. It extended from the common pasture land, through the Ryelands to the river and adjourned on the south the common meadow land (see fig. 30). Part of this field: the Thornditch Wong and the Ryelands Wong, were included in the vicarial glebe and had been enclosed by the vicar, Rev. Walter Kinnersley, a year or so previously c1608.

From witnesses' accounts it seems clear that various other freeholders followed his example, and by 1700 these closes are specifically mentioned: Barton Close, the Flatts (a block of closes near the site of the Nether Field and may have been part of it), Field Close Home Corner, Broadgate Close, Hassock Close, Flitter Close, Combs Close, Dufcote Close and Brook Close. A few of these, namely Field Close, Broadgate Close and Brook Close, were enclosed arable land, which may have formed part of the East or Tottle Brook Field, but the remainder were enclosed for pasture.

In order to preserve the three field system, it became necessary to re-divide the remaining two fields. The northerly parts of the West or Church Field and the East or Tottle Brook Field were separated to form the third or Far Field. It is interesting to note that this field was sometimes known as Steppa Field or Steopoe Furlong. Many old Bestonians recall the 'Devil Steps', a path leading from this field, and originally part of the field, which went to Wollaton. It is probable that this was a derivative of the older name for the field.

Further early enclosures are revealed by the 1806/9 Tithe Award Map, namely the Gleadwongs, the Heanings, the Musco Sykes group (including the Hopper Close), a few scattered parts of the Far Field near the Bramcote boundary: Long Close, Toad Close, Bramcote Nook Close and Bramcote Field Close; a few in the Tottle Brook Field: Stoneylands Close and Combs Close. Thus it may be seen that the villagers were being prepared for a full enclosure, which eventually took place in 1806.

2. The Civil War 1642-49

In the years prior to 1642 there was a growing resentment against Charles I over the imposition of Ship Money and the collection of forced loans. In March 1641/2 a Protestation was made by MP's and later by males over 18 years of age against the King's popish practices and the curtailment of the powers and privileges of Parliament. We are fortunate to have the full list of those who made their Protestation in Beeston. It shows 91 names, (see Appendix 7 on page 85) including many of the families who were noted earlier at the time of the Plague in 1593/4. The only name which appears to be missing is that of John Roe, whose wife was a Roman Catholic.

The following months were to bring an increasing rift between the King and Parliament, and although the villagers may have been unaware of much of this, the news of the King's attempts to seize arms and ammunition from Nottingham would certainly become known. The chief promoter of Parliament's interests in the county was Henry Ireton from nearby Attenborough, and he must have been familiar to Beeston folk. In June 1642 he was nominated as Captain of the horse troop of the forces of Nottingham. In July Charles decided to test the loyalty of his subjects by the solemn unfurling of his standard. Nottingham seemed to be in a strategic position for this and so on Friday, 19th August, Charles arrived here from Coventry. In all probability he would have passed through our area to reach the town and would have been seen by some of the Beeston folk as he was accompanied by 800 horse and various lords and ladies of the county! The standard was duly raised about 6.00pm on 22nd August and for a few days thereafter, but the response was poor – under 300 men enlisted! It was harvest time and most people were busy in their fields. It is doubtful if any Beeston men joined the King's army. Their sympathies would probably have been with the Parliamentary side and the local leaders, Henry Ireton and Nicholas Charlton of Chilwell Hall.

31. Raising the Standard (1642 woodcut)

By September 1642 Ireton had gathered his troop of horse and joined the Parliamentary army under the Earl of Essex, where he fought at Edgehill, Gainsborough, Bristol and Marston Moor. At the decisive battle of Naseby he was in command of the horse of the left wing. He was firm, brave, active, discreet and diligent. As a devout Puritan he was considered to be the best 'prayer-maker' and preacher in the Roundhead army. In 1646 he married Bridget, Oliver Cromwell's daughter and was highly regarded by his father-in-law.

Although no battles were fought in this area, Parliament's troops were moving across to attack the Royalist army based at Newark and there were frequent skirmishes in the defence of Nottingham and its castle from 1643. In May and June 1643 the united Parliamentary army, between five and six thousand, gathered in Nottingham to prevent the Queen joining the King in Newark. Unfortunately, part of this army made havoc and plunder in and around the town and this must surely have spread to Beeston. In any event, this great army would be seen as it assembled in the town. Cromwell is reputed to have stayed overnight at Attenborough, perhaps with Ireton's mother.

During the war, life in the village would have continued as normally as possible with the cultivation of the crops, etc. However, soldiers would have to be billeted and quartered as the need arose and they would have been able to claim crops and food. Meantime, taxation continued as previously and was compulsory for all except the poorest. Normally the village constable (Anthony Shrigley) would have been responsible for its collection in money or goods, but during the War, solders from their local headquarters would have collected in the village. Although we have no actual record of Beeston's taxes, it is known that in 1644 the Royalist garrison at Shelford were collecting taxes from Toton[1] so it is possible that they collected from Beeston also. Wollaton Hall nearby was garrisoned by

32. Henry Ireton's House, Attenborough

45

Parliamentary foot in 1643 and later the Willoughby family paid £793 for their protection to Parliament. Nobles and gentry were expected to pay large sums to support their cause.

During the War, the vicar of Beeston, Rev. Walter Kynnersley, died in c1644/5, and Rev. William Westoby was appointed in his place. He was specially commended for being 'a godly, honest and painfull minister, well affected towards Parliament'. As such, he was able to benefit from an augmentation to his living of £50, which Parliament authorised to certain needy livings. William Westoby seems to have retained his office until his death in 1658.

Parish registers had to be kept but very few entries were recorded during the War and no marriages from 1643-53. It is obvious that the uncertainty of the times made people very cautious about making binding contracts until there was more stability in the country.

33. Henry Ireton (1611- 1651)

The Protectorate 1649-1660

During this time the Puritans and Presbyterians organised themselves into voluntary presbyteries, taking over the livings of the episcopal clergy. In Beeston they appointed William Cross when William Westoby died, and he remained until his ejection at the Restoration in 1662. He was a good preacher and generally respected in the village. There were complaints, however, that the chancel of the church was not kept in good repair. Thomas Charlton of Chilwell was appointed as magistrate and authorised to conduct marriage ceremonies as civil contracts: there were only two during this time. Thomas Brighton of Beeston was officially appointed as Parish Register.

Meantime, Henry Ireton received high office in the government and was considered to be of great influence on Cromwell, who had hoped he might succeed him. He was appointed Lord Deputy of Ireland and sent to subdue the uprising there in 1651. After the seige of Limerick he caught the plague and died on 20th November. He was buried with honour in Henry VII's chapel at Westminster Abbey, but at the Restoration his body was removed and gibbeted at Tyburn. Henry's brother, John, became Lord Mayor of London in 1658 and was knighted by Cromwell. At the Restoration he was imprisoned in the Scilly Isles and died in 1689.

3. The Growth of Transport I : The Turnpike Roads*

With the developments in industry and trade in the seventeenth and eighteenth centuries it was necessary for improvements to be made in the roads. For centuries, the roads, hardly more than rough tracks, which linked Beeston to Nottingham and to nearby villages remained unaltered, being a sea of mud in winter and deeply rutted in summer. By a statute of 1555 each parish was ordered to appoint a surveyor of highways with power to call on available labour

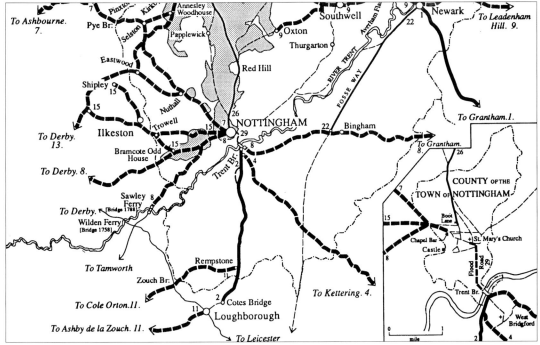

34. Turnpike roads around Nottingham

to work on the roads. By an act of Parliament in 1563, each villager was to give six days unpaid labour each year and the surveyor had powers to levy highway rates of up to 6d in the pound. We have no record of a highway surveyor in Beeston for this period, and it is obvious that standards of road maintenance were very low. By the late seventeenth and early eighteenth century it was reported that the roads through the Abbey lands (Beeston Lane) and through Beeston and Chilwell were in a ruinous condition, being narrow and dangerous for passengers. It was impossible for two coaches to pass each other.

In 1758 local landowners: Richard Strey (Lord of the Manor), Nicholas Strey, John Egginton, Thomas Charlton (Lord of the Manor, Chilwell), and others gained permission from Parliament to form a **Turnpike Trust.** It was authorised to erect bars at intervals along the roads and levy tolls at them which could then be spent on maintenance and rebuilding. Definite measurements were enforced for the widths of the new roads and turnpike labour of 3-6 days per year was compulsory for all able-bodied males, or a cash payment in lieu.

The first Turnpike Act of 1758/9 inaugurated the Nottingham to Derby road which passed through the fields in the northern part of the village, on the line of the present Derby Road. Milestones were erected at intervals and an original milestone may be seen today between the Wollaton Hall Lodge and the Beeston boundary. A second Turnpike Act inaugurated a branch of this road which led through the Abbey

35. Milestone on Derby Road

47

lands (Beeston Lane) to the village itself, on the line of the present Broadgate and High Road, and continued through Chilwell and Long Eaton to Sawley Ferry. In 1779 it was necessary to renew the Act for the completion of the work. An early map of Beeston (1774 by Chapman) shows Beeston Lane and part of the present High Road section completed, while the Broadgate section is merely a footpath. Only two houses were shown on this road: one may be the Greyhound Inn. The rest of the houses are firmly built around the old streets: Middle Street, Nether Street, the City and West End.

36. Part of Chapman's Map, 1776

Tolls were imposed on all types of carriages, horses, droves of cattle and sheep, but foot passengers travelled free. The inhabitants of Beeston and Chilwell were granted free passage for their animals and carriages in consideration of a payment by the Overseers of the Poor of ten shillings per year, in advance. As a result of these improved roads, new bridges were built to replace ferries or fords, etc. The one over the Tottle Brook at the Nottingham-Beeston boundary was built in 1792 at a cost of £12! Sawley Ferry was superseded by the Harrington Bridge under the Act of 1787/8.

*Much of the information in this section comes from Arthur Cossons, *Turnpike Roads of Nottinghamshire*, recently reprinted by Nottinghamshire County Council. Arthur Cossons, the father of Sir Neil Cossons, was Headmaster of Church Street School here for many years and did a great deal of research into the history of our area and to whom we owe a tremendous debt.

4. The Growth of Transport II : The Building of the Beeston Canal

For centuries, the River Trent had been used for the transportation of commodities: lead, copper, coal, salt and cheese from Cheshire and Staffordshire were passed down to its mouth at Hull,[2] while cargoes up the river included timber, hemp and flax from the Baltic and Norway, and also iron, malt and corn. Unfortunately, the river presented difficulties in navigation with shallows, currents and floods to be contended with as well as the narrow arches of the old Trent Bridge at Nottingham. Thus it is not surprising that, after the success of the Bridgwater Canal in 1761 and the subsequent building in 1777 of the Trent and Mersey Canal up to Shardlow, near Derby, that efforts should be made to improve the navigability of the Trent in this area.

37. Stagecoach travel

Consequently, in 1777 William Jessop, the engineer responsible for the Trent-Mersey Canal, surveyed the Trent and recommended that certain cuts should be made to facilitate this. One was to be at Meadow Lane in Nottingham to avoid the narrow arches at Trent Bridge and to connect with Lenton and thence to Langley Mill. The other, and more important for Beeston, was to construct a canal from the village to join the Nottingham Canal at Lenton and thus bypass the dangerous shallows at Clifton Bend and at Wilford. In 1783 the Trent Navigation Company was formed for the express purpose of improving the river and William Jessop was appointed as engineer. The company acquired the powers to construct the canal as Jessop had envisaged.

This was a major engineering feat involving the use of gangs of itinerant navigators ('navvies' for short) using chiefly shovels and wheelbarrows. It is estimated that each man raised about 20 tons each day! In doing so, they trod the clay at the bottom of the cut, thus forming an impervious lining. These gangs of navvies were recruited from far afield and developed a distinctive dress and customs which alienated them from the local community,

38. William Jessop

39. Plan of canals around Nottingham

40. Lockkeeper's House, Beeston Canal

41. Beeston Canal

who viewed their general licentiousness and drunkenness with horror! However, they performed a great task here and the cost of the canal at £80,000 was amply repaid by the increase in traffic and the ability of the barges to carry heavier loads of goods from the industrial Midlands to almost every part of Britain.

The canal was entered from the western side by two locks set at right angles – the eastern one connected with the canal itself, while the southern one enabled boats to enter the Trent below the weir and use the shallow waters by Wilford if they wished. This back lock has been closed for many years, but it is possible to see its location today.

42. Lock Cottages, Beeston Canal

At the entrance to the locks a set of workers' houses were built. The main and earliest one overlooking the passenger bridge is especially fine and was built for the lock-keeper. It was his duty to collect the tolls from the passing barges and boats, and to keep account of their cargoes. The lonely situation of the canal in 1796, the nearest house then was number 19 Dovecote Lane, the former Goat Inn, made it imperative for the lock-keeper to be given some protection. Accordingly, he was supplied with a blunderbuss to fire in case of trouble, and a cutlass. Both these articles were still lodged in the lock-keeper's house until a few years ago, and have now been placed in a canal museum, probably in Gloucester.[3]

As traffic through the canal increased, so it became necessary to provide facilities for the bargees and boatmen. By the early nineteenth century two inns had been built: the Jolly Anglers by the canal side and a little further away the Boat and Horses. Eventually about 1830 a small community grew up in this area called the Rylands.

5. The Beginnings of the Hosiery Industry in Beeston

In 1589 William Lee of Calverton, Nottinghamshire, invented the stocking frame for the production of machine knitted hose. After Lee's death in France in 1610, his brother James brought his machines back into this area and the framework knitting industry was established. By the 1690s there were framework knitters in Beeston. The earliest mention we have is of Barnham West in 1698, but there must have been others. During the period 1700-40 41 framework knitters were working here and the number increased

43. Framework Knitter's Machine

through the century.

The industry was domestic based and involved most of the family. The frame, a very heavy and complicated piece of machinery, was operated by the father or one of the sons, while the womenfolk would be responsible for the seaming of the hose and the spinning of the yarn. The children could comb and card the yarn. Maximum light was essential for the production of the hose, which must be free from faults, and so the upper rooms of houses were adapted by the provision of long windows and most stocking frames were positioned there. Beeston had a number of these framework knitters' houses, some were to be found on Middle Street until the 1950s, others may still be seen in Bramcote and Stapleford today. The building and repair of the frames led to skilled mechanics becoming framesmiths and setters-up.

44. Domestic scene, Framework Knitter's Cottage

The marketing of the finished hose was done by agents who travelled round the area collecting the goods and providing the yarn for further goods. Rich businessmen employed these agents, rented the frames to the workers and paid them for the hose. These men were called 'hosiers'. By the mid eighteenth century, one of these hosiers, Joseph Holland, had already taken up residence in Beeston and was playing a prominent part in village life.[4]

During this century there is evidence that the character of the village was changing. Members of old-established farming families: Levis, Smalley, Lacey and West, were turning to the new industry. There is also evidence of an increase in population, due perhaps to men coming into the village as framework knitters.

Sources (Chapter Seven)
[1]*Rentals for Toton, 1644*, Nottingham Archives Office
[2]*Beeston Canal*, City of Nottingham publication
[3]Evidence given by lock-keeper who found them
[4]*Beeston Parish Register*

45. Stockingers' Cottages, Derby Road, Bramcote

CHAPTER EIGHT

Rev. Timothy Wylde and his Commonplace Book

Rev. Timothy Wylde was Vicar of Beeston from September 1758 until his death in January 1799: a span of over 40 years and the longest serving vicar here. He has given us an interesting and colourful picture of himself and the parish through his 'commonplace books' or diary, which was re-discovered in 1985 after lingering in a bank vault since 1916.

He was born at Woodhouse Eaves in Leicestershire on 11th November, 1705, the younger son of Thomas Wylde, who came originally from Nottingham. Timothy's elder brother, Isaac, became an apothecary in Bridlesmith Gate from about 1720, and later became Chamberlain and Mayor in 1759. Of Timothy's early life we know very little. He had no university education, but he was obviously a person of intelligence, with a great love of learning. It is quite possible that he may have studied at one of the dissenting academies with a view to entering the Non-conformist ministry. We know that he had a copy of Isaac Watts' hymns in his library, and he spent three years as a travelling preacher in Essex before going to London, when he decided to take holy orders in 1739.

It was during 1736 that he began his commonplace book, chiefly at first for the purpose of keeping an accurate account of his finances. This was always a matter of some concern to him and it is particularly from the most detailed items of income and expenditure that we are able to gain so much knowledge of his way of life. Part of the earlier entries are written in a simple form of shorthand (invented by John Byron) which was beginning to be used in the eighteenth century. This may have been to hide his financial transactions from prying eyes and indeed to make certain facts quite confidential, some of the earlier pages have been carefully cut out.

In 1741 he was appointed as Chaplain and Steward of the Hospital of St. Cross at Winchester, where he was required to furnish his own apartments. He gives us details of good bought (damask tablecloths, china cups and saucers, teapot, glasses, corner cupboard, large dining table, three Windsor chairs, fine quality towels and sheets together with kitchen utensils) which show a desire for gracious living; for which his salary of £70-80 per annum with extras would allow. He had time there for leisure activities: the bowling green at Winchester was a favourite venue, and the betting and gambling places of the town, though here he was often on the losing side! He loved fine clothes and was prepared to spend a great deal on them, and for them to be washed and mended regularly.

Already he was becoming something of a connoisseur of food and wines and took an interest in home brewing, where a recipe for making mead took prominence. Above all, the period from 1741 to 1752 must have seen the beginning of his acquisition of a fine collection of books, which were to be so valuable in his future career. Fortunately for us, Timothy, with his characteristic thoroughness, allocated 17 pages of the diary to a complete catalogue of over 200 books, together with their cost. From this list we can see the wide range of his interests: not only were there the usual devotional and theological works, but also Greek, Latin and

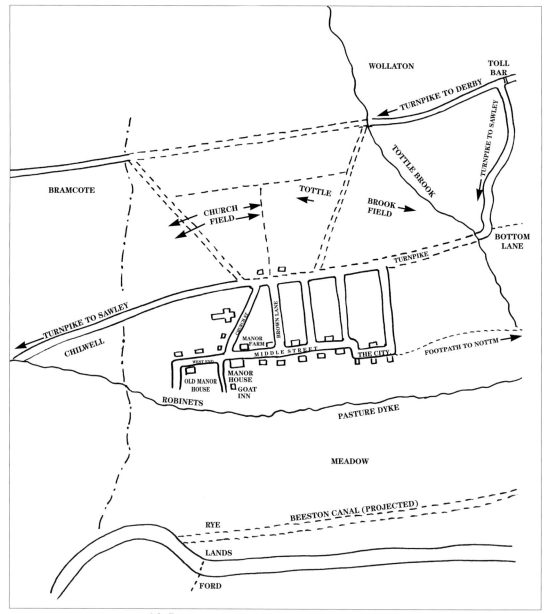

46. Beeston, about 1776 (from Chapman's Map)

Hebrew dictionaries, grammars and texts, Bacon's Essays, Newton's Chronology, Boyle's lectures, Whiston's Euclid, etc. Whether at this time Timothy was able to gain any experience in teaching is uncertain, but it was quite usual for clergymen to take private pupils for tuition, and this may explain the acquisition of the classical texts in which he must have received a good grounding earlier.

In 1752 he left Winchester to become Under Master of the Free Grammar School at Coventry and Lecturer (ie Curate) of St. John's Church there. The six years spent there were to pave the way for his future advancement, for in August 1758 he was appointed as Master of the Free

54

School in Nottingham, and in September he was inducted into the benefice of Beeston. For a number of years it had been the custom for the Master of the Free School to be appointed as Vicar of Beeston. As Master, he would be accommodated in the house attached to the School and not at the Vicarage in Beeston. This was fortunate, for the Vicarage was dilapidated, built of 'mud and stud' and thatched, and appears to have dated from the fifteenth century!

It is of Timothy's work as Vicar of Beeston that his diary and the parish registers reveal most. Here he proved himself as methodical and conscientious as in the scholastic sphere, and showed above all a care and concern for his parishioners, which they were quick to appreciate. From one of them, recalling him years later, we learn of his pleasant appearance, his height of 5 ft 8 ins, and his hair worn in a queue pigtail, as was the

47. Timothy Wylde's Book

fashion of those days. He would be found in his place every Sunday and often in the village on Saturday too. During his first year here (1758-9) he recorded spending £4 1s on horse hire: a large sum out of a living of £39! From the diary we find every item of rent, tithe and dues he received from Beeston from 1758-64 meticulously recorded. Not only this, but the names of the persons are shown, together with the crops etc. they brought as 'tithes', as in the following examples:

48. Nottingham Free Grammar School, 1750

49. The Old Vicarage, Beeston (demolished 1860)

				£	s	d
1759	Mar	24	year's small tithe – Henry Cox		4	0
	April	14	year's rent – Wm. Holmes	4	6	6
			+ tithe of eggs	4	4	
		16	Recd. Thos. Cross – tithe of apples			
			(9 pecks)		2	0
	May	5	Pig (3/-) + Easter dues (2/-) E. Marriott		5	0
	June	16	year's dues - Wilkinson 3/9			
			+ tithe of potatoes 1/3		5	0
1764	April	7	Mr. Wilkinson for tithes of 20 lambs,			
			5 cows, 1 foal		4	0
		29	Mr. Cox's Lammas dues 8/-			
			+ tithe of turnips 5/6		13	6

Likewise, in the matter of fees for Banns, Churchings, Marriages, Baptisms and Burials, the names of the persons are noted. The entries reveal infant mortality rates and deaths of women in childbirth. The parish registers too came under his meticulous care with his fine, clear handwriting – not for him was the task delegated to curate or parish clerk until 1796 when he was almost 92! Here, especially from 1777 onwards, he would give interesting details of some of the persons concerned, often showing his sympathy with the afflicted, eg:

> 1777, Alice Smith, daughter of Joseph Cockayne, died of consumption, aged 29; 1781, Seven folk died of epidemic flux; 1783, William Whitacre killed by falling off an Hovell astride an upright post, aged 48; 1788, Robert Hardy, a soldier, died; 1794, Wm. son of Sarah Saxton. This child was taken out of a necessary house of John Toplis, Peck Lane about 10th June last; 1795, Elizabeth Smith died in Gedling workhouse; 1796, James Marshall - an aged shepherd died.

Until 1794, entries in the registers were subject to government tax, much to Timothy's disgust. When the Act was repealed, Timothy was led to exclaim in the register *"Farewell, Lord John and his shabby tax says Mr. Wilde"*. An interesting fact lies behind an entry made in 1782. It says, *"October 20th – Elizabeth, daughter of Mary Read – an illegitimate – was baptized, for which Mary did public penance, coming into church barefoot and clad in a white sheet."* This appears to have been one of the last such acts to have been recorded in the country and the child's baptism in church may well have been due to Timothy's influence. (Incidentally, Elizabeth grew up and became the wife of a later Vicar of Beeston!).

Throughout, Timothy's diary shows his kindness to poor folk and to those who worked for him. Timothy himself was cared for from 1759-64 by his housekeeper, Ann Hill. On 7th March, 1765 Timothy (then 59) and Ann (38) were married at St. Mary's Church, Nottingham and in 1766 a son, Thomas, was born and baptized there on 9th May.

In 1793 he resigned as Master of the Free School, having given many years of good teaching and organised the modern side of the school to help less academic pupils. He was granted a pension of £70 per year by the Corporation, and he went to live on High Pavement. He continued as Vicar of Beeston until his death in January 1799, having (as the Nottingham Journal says) *"retained all his faculties until within a day or two of his dissolution"* (See Appendix 8 on page 86). He was buried in St. Peter's Church, where there is a commemorative plaque on the floor of the south aisle to Timothy and his wife.

During his long years as Vicar, Timothy would have seen many changes. The increase in the framework knitting industry brought more workers into the village. There was a need for more houses to accommodate them so that by 1790 there were 150 houses in the village. The building of the turnpike road through Beeston encouraged new houses to be built along that road. There was some evidence of rich people coming from Nottingham and erecting houses here: Joseph Salthouse, a jeweller and mercer built his house on Broadgate and called it "Dagfa House".

Timothy would have been moved by the plight of the poor, especially the widows left without support. It was during his time that the Poor Row was built by the church and allocated to widows, who could live there rent free. In 1777 a workhouse was built in the City to accommodate 12 poor persons. Stocks of material would be kept by the parish and the able-bodied poor would be taught to spin, card and weave.

During this period, John Wesley was travelling and preaching in the area and before the end of the century, Methodist societies were to be found in Stapleford and Chilwell. That there was no Methodist witness here before 1798 was due to the influence and example of Timothy Wylde. He worked tirelessly preaching and teaching his flock and caring for them as a true Christian pastor should.

50. Dagfa House, Broadgate

CHAPTER NINE

Nineteenth Century Beeston and the Industrial Revolution

1. The Enclosure Act

In 1806 an Act was passed for the enclosing of lands in the parish of Beeston. Two commissioners were appointed: these were to be surveyors or land agents from another part of the county and were Jonas Bettison and John Bailey. In 1809 these commissioners, having surveyed the parish, stated that the land to be enclosed was 822 acres, to be made tithe free and ancient enclosed lands and homesteads liable to tithe was 687 acres 2 roods 29 perches.

Their first concern was the roads and their widths. The Nottingham to Derby Turnpike was fixed at 50 feet, the Sawley Turnpike through Beeston was fixed at 40 feet and Cowgate (Wollaton Road) at 30 feet. Bridle paths and footways were designated as were drains and watercourses and the scouring of ditches, etc. Certain areas of land were allocated to individuals as previous owners of tithe rights, etc. The Vicar was given 8 acres for his glebe and 66 acres for his tithe, Henry Cavendish 97 acres for his corn and grain tithe, Rev. P. S. Broughton for his hay tithe had 54 acres and the poor of Beeston were given 7 acres in the Hassock Close. The rest of the land was allocated to 48 owners in Beeston according to several rights of common, and any land remaining was available for sale. Owners were expected to plant hedges around their land and thus the village had a very different appearance after the Act was implemented.

The detailed survey revealed a wealth of old field and footpath names which show some of the Scandinavian or Danish origin. The chief advantage to the village at this time was the availability of land for sale. Thus, when in 1819 Henry Kirkland from Nottingham wanted land to expand his lace manufacturing business and found none available there, he was able to buy land in Beeston for his factory and his residence. Other lace manufacturers followed and thus helped to establish the lace trade in Beeston.

2. The Development of the Lace Trade

In the late eighteenth century the hosiery trade suffered a severe decline as fancy hose became less fashionable. In the meantime, lace in its many forms became very fashionable. As handmade lace was very expensive, skilled framework knitters experimented to make lace on their stocking frames, but without success. Eventually, about 1809, John Heathcoat devised a machine incorporating the stocking frame and a warp frame which was able to produce bobbin lace. About 1813 John Leavers

51. Former residence of Kirkland family, Broadgate

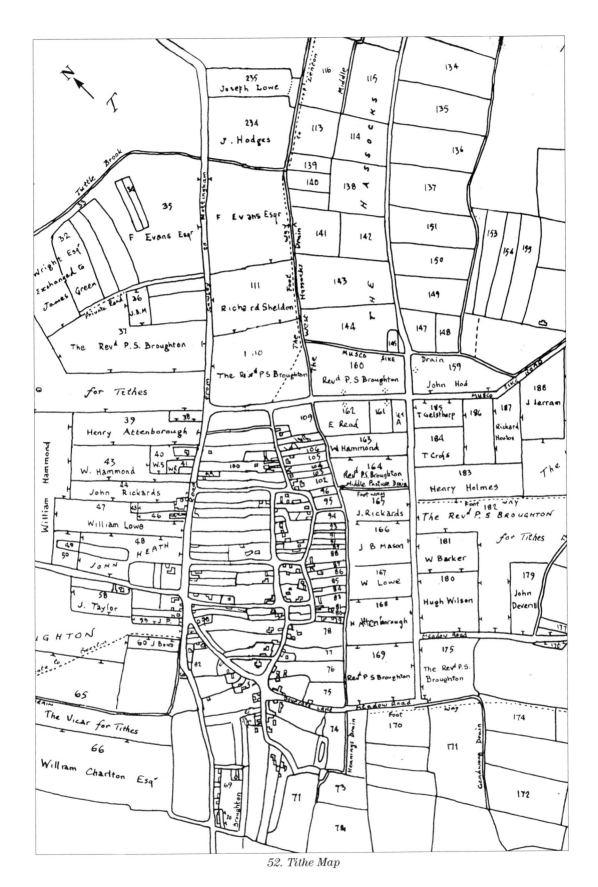

52. Tithe Map

developed this machine to produce 'fancy lace' which could be made in larger widths. More extensive premises were needed for some of these machines and as land was scarce in Nottingham, enterprising manufacturers sought land elsewhere.

By 1809, Beeston had its Enclosure Act and had land for sale. In 1819, Henry Kirkland, a manufacturer in Nottingham, bought land here on Moore Gate and built his factory, the first lace factory in Beeston. It can still be seen today as the building adjoining the Alexon premises on Middle Street, at present unoccupied. By 1825 he employed over 100 people. Meanwhile, other manufacturers were using three or four machines in small sheds or in their homes. These wooden

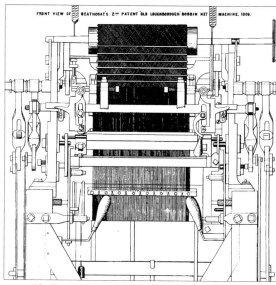

53. Heathcote's Bobbin Net Machine, 1809

machines could be worked by hand, and were to be found particularly in the Villa Street and Chapel Street areas. After 1834 Henry Kirkland and others were adding a jacquard attachment

54. Henry Kirkland's Lace Factory

to their machines to produce patterning, and there was a necessity to build larger factories.

The number of machines in the village grew rapidly between 1826-36 from 69 to 202. A corresponding increase in population was seen from 1,534 in 1821, 2,530 in 1831 and 2,807 by 1844. By 1841, two-thirds of the working population were employed in textile manufacture. In the 1830s another factory was built, this time in Cross Street. This was later to be known as Dobson's Mill, or the Bank Factory, and by the 1850s was used

by Thomas Elliott employing about 60 men. About the same time, William Vickers of Nottingham built a small factory on a site on Albion Street, which was later taken over by William Felkin (author of *A History of Machine Wrought Hosiery and Lace Manufacturers*) and his sons William and Robert. They had 92 machines there, which were powered

55. Swiss Mills, Beeston

56. Anglo-Scotian Mills, Beeston

by steam about 1840, but the firm had disappeared in Beeston by 1871.

In the adjoining Villa Street, by 1841 Thomas Pollard, formerly from Chilwell, was working three or four wooden machines by hand in small premises. However, in 1865 he was joined by his son John and by the 1870s this son was able to purchase the Bank Factory and the one attached to it. In 1886 John built the large Swiss Mills factory on Wollaton Road, with standings for 75 machines, which he was able to let out to various small manufacturers. During the century, the lace trade had its ups and downs, but the population increased gradually to 3,134 in 1871.

However, change was to come with the arrival of Frank Wilkinson from Hucknall. He was originally a manufacturer of Shetland shawls, mantles and scarves and had called his firm the Anglo-Scotian works and this name continued when he took over the Beeston site. In 1874 he took over the derelict factory of the Felkins and extended it to house his first lace curtain machines. He added buildings in front and towards the Poplars and finally a bleach yard and power house. The whole site now covered two acres and the buildings were to house all the processes in lace curtain manufacture, from designing, manufacture, bleaching, dressing to packaging and despatch; as well as the production of lace and Shetland shawls. By 1886 the firm was employing 1,000 hands, when a disastrous fire demolished the buildings. A new building with further improvements was erected but, alas! six years later this too was partly demolished by a second fire. The present Victorian Gothic building was erected in 1892/3, the ornate entrance on Albion Street supposedly modelled on Thrumpton Hall. The factory continued to expand with employees coming from a wide area around Beeston. Other Wilkinson factories were opened in Chilwell, Borrowash and the United States. Unfortunately, Frank Wilkinson, a great entrepreneur, died in August 1897, and the whole enterprise went into liquidation the following year. Eventually the Anglo-Scotian complex was purchased by John Pollard and run as a tenement factory into the next century.

Smaller lace firms continued to flourish throughout the century, occupying small premises or renting parts of the larger factories. Machine builders were very necessary to provide new machines or repair old ones, and a number set up in Beeston. The blacksmiths were also important, as transport by horse and cart was still common.

57. Blacksmith's House and Smithy at rear

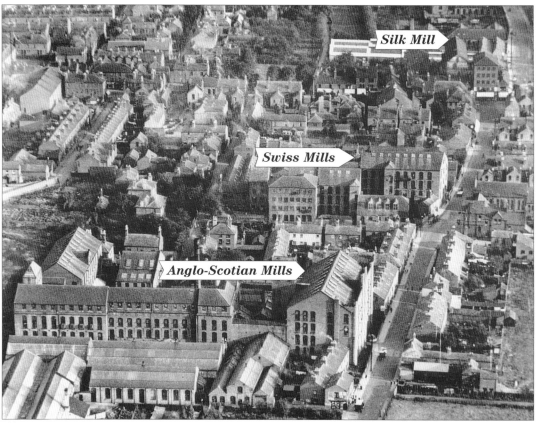

58. *Aerial view of Beeston showing mills, c.1928*

The Silk Industry

In 1826 William Lowe erected a silk mill on the turnpike. It was a companion mill to one at Derby and appears to have dealt mainly with silk throwstering. By 1831 it was employing about 200 people, when the Reform Bill rioters from Nottingham came and burnt down most of the building in protest at Mr. Lowe's opposition to the Bill. Much valuable high-class machinery was destroyed with a large quantity of silk, and the total damage was valued at £7,790. Mr. Lowe rebuilt the mill and in 1841 bequeathed it to Francis Gill, who later took John Watson into partnership. By 1851 the mill employed about 580 people and must have been the largest mill between here and Derby. Mr. Gill lived at the Grange and Mr. Watson on the turnpike in a house later known as the Constitutional Club. The machines appear to have been steam powered, using the water from a large reservoir situated on Brown

59. *The Ten Bell*

60. *Part of the original Humber Works, Humber Road*

Lane (Station Road) behind Shaw and Marvin's works, from where remains of the reservoir fitments have been discovered. The mill site covered a large area, with subsidiary buildings for the mill manager, etc.

Mr. Gill founded a school for girls in the mill and the teacher was Miss Cowell. On the factory roof was the bell which called folk to work and scholars to their lessons, and also acted as the fire bell. This bell may now be seen on Stoney Street, outside Sainsbury's store, having been donated by its former owner, John Pollard, who bought it after 1902 when the Silk Mill closed.

Since then the Mill has had a number of uses. Part of it on the ground floor was used for our first cinema, whilst other rooms housed furniture, warehouses, etc. Latterly the building has become derelict and the older parts were demolished in 1992.

61. *Humber bicycle*

Further Industrial Developments in the Nineteenth Century

In Chilwell, John Pearson had established a large nursery and seed warehouse by 1844. In 1845, his son, Henry, joined Robert Foster of Beeston to found the firm of Foster and Pearson, which made horticultural buildings and boilers for their greenhouses. In 1888 Henry Pearson and his brother, Louis, formed the Beeston Foundry Company in Brown Lane. In 1897 the firm transferred to new premises on Queen's Road adjoining the railway and became the Beeston Boiler Company, producing domestic boilers for customers all over the world.

In 1875, Thomas Humber and his partners set up a small bicycle factory on the present GPT site (the Nelson Works) and employed about 80 men. About 1887 he bought land on Humber Road and Queen's Road on which he erected a large factory for the manufacture of more up-to-date cycles and later for motor cycles. In 1903, he

62. *Former Flour Mill, Derby Street*

produced the Beeston car and by this time the firm employed over 2,000 people.

The malting industry increased during the century. In 1881 there were six maltings in the village with two near the station, one of which remains today. The hosiery industry continued with mechanisation and in 1898 Joseph Barlow established his firm for the production of half-hose. Small building firms were formed, one of which, founded in 1846 by Levi Hofton, continues today.

The Flour Mill
The flour mill was erected on the Turnpike at its junction with the present Derby Street in the early 1860s, when Mr. Peter Kirkby was named as the miller. In 1881 the mill (then known as Lawn Mills) was taken over by Wm. & George King, who were provision merchants with shops in Wheeler Gate and Lister Gate in Nottingham. They are mentioned as millers here in 1885/6 but not thereafter. It seems likely that the mill was steam powered.

In 1898-9 the premises were in use as the Beeston Steam Laundry and later by the Shaftesbury Laundry. More recently, they were used by a curtain making firm and are now part of Smith's Garden Centre.

All these commercial activities required banking facilities and in 1883 the Nottingham Joint Stock bank was opened here and has now become the Midland Bank with premises in the Square since 1905.

The War Memorials
During the 19th century, England was involved in both the Crimean War (1854-56) and the South African or Boer War (1899-1902). Beeston men were among those killed there and memorials were erected by public subscription to commemorate them. The Crimean War Memorial was erected in 1857 and stands in the churchyard.

The Boer War Memorial depicting *Hope* was unveiled on 13 February 1904 and stood in the Square in front of the Council Offices (see fig. 81, p.75). Since the redevelopment of the Square, this memorial has been placed outside the entrance to the Broadgate Recreation Ground.

The Great War (1914-18) and World War II (1939-45) armed services casualties are commemorated on the War Memorial at the junction of Middle Street and Dovecote Lane.

63. Crimea War Memorial

3. The Growth of Transport III : The Coming of the Railway
The Midland Counties Railway was formed in 1836 and the first section of the line to be built was to be that of Nottingham to Derby. It was to pass through Beeston on land to the south of the main village, which was owned by Richard Harwood, the licensee of the 'Boat and Horses' Inn and a farmer in Beeston Meadow. Consequently, on 13th August, 1838 Mr. Harwood laid

64. Beeston Station, 1839

65. Beeston Station, 1996

the first block of the Beeston section of the railway on his meadow land. On 30th May, 1839 the Nottingham to Derby railway was opened with a station at Beeston. At first there were four trains each way, from Nottingham at 7.00am, 11.00am, 3.00pm and 7.00pm and from Derby at 8.00am, 12 noon, 4.30pm and 8.00pm. On 5th May, 1840 the line to Leicester via the Iron Bridge over the Trent and the tunnel at the Redhill at Ratcliffe on Soar was opened. On 9th March, 1840 the Victoria Hotel adjoining the station was opened. In 1847 an enlarged station building was erected and is still in use today. By 1853 trains were running to London, Sheffield, Lincoln, etc.

66. Railway Carriages, 1839

The railway played an important part in the development of local industries as manufacturers took advantage of the improved facilities to send their goods by rail. Some Nottingham business men took up residence in the southern part of Beeston from whence they could commute to Nottingham each day. The frequency of trains grew from 50 per day in 1874, over 75 in 1881 and 110 passenger trains east and west each weekday in 1889. The proximity of the railway to the village encouraged other industries to come to this area, so that their goods could be transported quickly and efficiently all over the country. This greater use of the railway by the 1890s encouraged the development of the Rylands area, which has continued into this century.

4. The Growth of Nonconformity

Beeston does not appear to have been influenced by John Wesley during his many visits to Nottingham from 1741-88. Probably this was due to the influence of the vicar, Rev. Timothy Wylde, who was a caring pastor of the flock. However, after his death in 1799, both the Methodist and the Baptist causes began in the village.

67. Methodist New Connexion Chapel

The Development of the Methodist Church

In 1798 the New Connexion Methodists from Chilwell began preaching in the streets and soon a small society was formed. Persecution was encountered, but the group persisted and soon obtained the use of a barn which was registered for worship on 26th August, 1799. In 1805 a small chapel was built.

About this time too, William Maltby, a Wesleyan Methodist, moved to Beeston and gathered a small group together. Then in 1819, Henry Kirkland and his wife came to Beeston from Radford, and they were Wesleyan Methodists. Henry set up his lace factory in Moore Gate and soon encouraged others to join the Methodist cause. In 1821, the New Connexion Methodists having declined, the Wesleyan Methodists were able to buy the 1805 chapel for £120. This soon became too small for them, and so land was bought further down Chapel Street and a new chapel was built in 1825. In 1830 this was rebuilt to accommodate

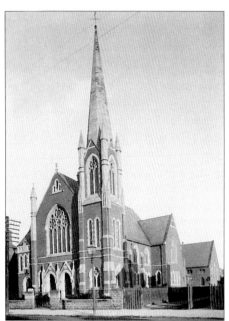

68. Wesleyan Methodist Church, Chilwell Road (c.1920)

larger numbers. By 1898, this chapel had over 200 members and a large Sunday School, so plans were made to erect a larger building on a prominent site on Chilwell Road. The trustees decided to inaugurate a public competition for a design for the new building, and this was won by Mr. W. J. Morley of Bradford. It is of Victorian Gothic design throughout both the church and the adjoining school building. The whole is dominated by a tall spire, which is a landmark for the area. The church had accommodation for 750 people (rather less today due to some minor alterations internally). There is a fine three manual organ given by Mr. William Roberts, one of the trustees. The building was opened for worship on 29th May, 1902 at a cost of £9,000.

Meantime, in 1829 the New Connexion Methodists had revived and were able to build a new chapel in Chapel Street and in 1896 opened new school premises. About 1850 the Primitive Methodists who had been worshipping in a cottage from about 1820, took over a former Baptist chapel on Wollaton Road, which was enlarged in 1882 and is still in active use today.

A small group calling themselves the Wesley Reformers broke away from the Wesleyan Methodists in Chapel Street and began meeting at the old Commercial Inn. By 1853, possibly with the aid of a local lace manufacturer, Thomas Elliott, they were able to buy land on Willoughby Street and erected their Ebenezer-Free Methodist chapel there. In 1907 the New Connexion Methodists and the Free Methodists joined to form the United Methodist Church, and by 1915 they had decided to worship together at the Willoughby

69. Wollaton Road Methodist Church

Street premises, and the Chapel Street premises were sold in 1947. The Willoughby Street chapel was closed in 1964 during circuit re-organisation.

During the rapid growth of Beeston during the 1880s, and especially after the Humber factory was established, the Wesleyan Methodists in Chapel Street felt there was a need for a Sunday School in the Queen's Road area. Consequently, services and Sunday School began in the Mess Room of the Humber Works from about 1885. By 1886 a site was bought on Queen's Road and a Sunday School was built in 1887. A growing school and capacity congregations gave urgency to the building of a chapel there, which was opened in May 1900, and is in active use today.

About 1885, too, the religious revival of Moody and Sankey inspired some young men from the Wesleyan Chapel to start open air missions in Beeston. In 1888 they were able to buy the malt rooms on Union Street for their meetings and erected a building adjoining them for a mission hall, which was opened in 1912 as the Gospel Mission and is now known as the Oasis Christian Centre.

The Development of the Baptist Church

A few members of the General Baptist church in Nottingham were living in Beeston in 1803 and in Chilwell there were Baptists attending the Ilkeston church. In 1803, however, the Rev. Thomas Rogers moved to Beeston, taking up residence in part of the Manor House, now left vacant by the death of Mr. Richard Strey, the Lord of the Manor. Mr. Rogers established a small school there and gained permission to hold services in the schoolroom from 1st January, 1804.

70. Old Baptist Chapel, Nether Street

Soon a Baptist church in Beeston was authorised with the early members from Nottingham and Ilkeston as the foundation, and joined by new converts. In September 1805 land at Dead Man's Gardens was purchased and a small chapel 11 yards by 8 yards was erected and opened for worship on 24th August, 1806. New converts continued and in 1836 the chapel was enlarged.

About 1835 a small Particular Baptist church was built on Wollaton Road, on a site adjoining the Commercial Inn, and around 1841, 45 members of the Nether Street chapel joined it. However, after some years they returned, and the Particular Baptist church was sold to the Primitive Methodists.

Towards the end of the century, a number of Congregationalists were worshipping with the Baptists and as this number grew, it was decided to build a more convenient and beautiful building at which both denominations could worship. Land was obtained on Dovecote Lane and the new church, known as the Union Church, was opened in 1899 by the famous Baptist divine, Dr. John Clifford. Dr. Clifford was born in Sawley in 1836 but came to Beeston at the age of four and with his parents was associated with the Baptist Chapel on Nether Street, where he was baptized in 1851 and later preached his first sermon. After training at Leicester Theological College, he was appointed to Praed Street Baptist Chapel in London. Here he studied widely and became one of the foremost preachers and scholars. He had a special interest in education, championing the cause of undenominational state education and had a profound influence in England for his Christian views.

Today the Baptists have moved from Nether Street and now use the Union Church, which is re-named appropriately the John Clifford Memorial Church. Meantime, the Congregationalists built their own church on Boundary Road in 1933 and this is now known as the United Reformed Church.

71. Wesleyan Day School, 1839

5. Nineteenth Century Social Reforms

Local Government – Originally this was carried out through the Vestry Meeting, the Churchwardens, the Overseers of the Poor and the Surveyor of Roads, supervised by Justices of the Peace. In 1836 Beeston came under the Basford Poor Law Union for matters relating to the care of the poor. In 1858 Parliament passed a Local Government Act giving more power to the local communities and in 1872 Beeston set up a Local Board of Health comprising eight elected members to deal with Health and Sanitation primarily, but also to include care of the highways, public lighting and the collection of rates. The growth of population during the period and the provision of many new houses brought increased local administration through new bye-laws in 1881. By 1892, the Board had taken responsibility for the Fire Brigade and had issued rules and regulations for its members.

72. Church Street School, c.1930

In 1894 after a further Local Government Act, the Board was replaced by an Urban District Council with the Chairman of the Board, Mr. Benjamin Collington, becoming the first chairman of the new body. In 1897 the Council Offices were built in the Square, using the land of the old Pinfold, this being the only communal land apart from church property. These offices continued in use until the Town Hall was built in 1938.

Education – Originally there was no state education, but Beeston had some "private" academies and dame schools. The first school to be built was the National School in 1834. It was a church school, situated in Brown Lane (Station Road) and was one of the first to receive a Government grant under the new Act. In 1839 a Wesleyan Day School was started and in 1866 it moved into a new building adjoining the Wesleyan chapel on Chapel street.

In 1874 Education Act school boards were to be set up to provide undenominational education. In 1880 Beeston's school board of elected members was set up and in 1882 the first school was built in Church Street for 350 children, the cost being £5,241. This school was to

73. Nether Street Schools, c.1904

replace the National School, which became too small for the increased number of children. In 1893 this was enlarged to accommodate 950 children. In 1898 the Nether Street schools were built to provide for 1,000 children living in the southern part of the village. This school replaced the Wesleyan Day School whose pupils and Head Master transferred to the new premises and whose foundation stone had been laid by Dr. John Clifford. During the years this school has had many changes from all age school to secondary boys' and girls' school with adjoining infant school, and today is a large primary school with adjoining nursery school, which is now called the John Clifford School.

Other Social Changes – These were brought about by generous benefactors or other independent bodies. In 1875 Miss Catherine Bayley founded an orphanage here on Imperial Road. In 1897 Almshouses were erected by public subscription in Broughton Street. Friendly Societies were formed and the Loyal Nelson Lodge of the Independent Order of Oddfellows was meeting at the Star Inn from 1890. Benevolent societies were founded, often in connection with churches. The Wesleyan church had one founded in 1836, which has continued to the present day.

It is to the Methodist cause in Beeston and Chilwell that we owe a very precious heritage of a group of traditional carols, one or two of which appear to be unique to this area. These carols are sung regularly in the streets during the Christmas period by the Beeston Methodist Carol Choir and the money raised is given to the Benevolent Society mentioned above.

A library was founded in 1834 at the instigation of the vicar, Rev. John Wolley. It was a subscription library and quickly accumulated over 600 books, but it did not survive for many years. Unfortunately, Beeston did not have public library facilities until they were provided through the County Council in the 1930s.

CHAPTER TEN

The Twentieth Century

Industrial Changes

1. An Industrial Satellite of Nottingham

The expansion of the lace industry towards the end of the nineteenth century had already brought a period of prosperity to the village and the population had doubled between 1871 and 1891 to reach 6,948. Unfortunately, this showed little development in the hosiery industry where the manufacturers had dropped from five to two. (See Appendix 9 on page 86 for statistics relating to industrial growth during the 19th and 20th centuries).

However, there were already signs of new industries in the village when, in the 1880s, Humber, Marriott and Cooper (trading as the Nottingham Cycle Company) sought expansion and bought land here by the railway and built a factory for 80 workers. Later the larger Humber & Co. Cycle Company bought an imposing site at the junction of Queen's Road and New Lane (now Humber Road) and built a large factory which was soon to accommodate their 2,000 workers. By 1898, the firm was producing motor cars too, the first being called the 'Beeston' car. By 1900, the firm had expanded with factories in Coventry and Wolverhampton.

In 1897 the Beeston Boiler Co., founded by Foster and Pearson, moved to the Queen's Road and Mona Street area and built larger premises by the railway to cope with the increasing demand for their 'Beeston' and 'Robin Hood' boilers. With these and other developments, the population had increased to 8,960 by 1900. This necessitated much additional housing, especially in the Queen's Road area.

The dawn of the new century saw increasing productivity from the aforementioned firms. Meantime, the lace trade had varying fortunes: Pollard's Swiss Mills continued to flourish and were extended to accommodate additional machines. Frank Wilkinson's Anglo-Scotian Mills were taken over eventually by Pollard, after Wilkinson's firm went into liquidation in 1898 and was let out to various tenants. The lace curtain industry continued with A. & F. H. Parkes in the Anglo-Scotian premises from 1904/5, together with Widdowson and Truman in their new Falcon Works on Station Road and Wm. Emmett in their small factory off Station Road. Unfortunately, there was a steady decline in the workings of the Silk Mill, which finally closed in 1902.

Already, however, there were further signs of diversification when in 1901 the National Telephone Company opened a small factory on the one acre site by the railway formerly used by Humber, Marriott and Cooper. By 1903 this firm had been taken over by British L.M. Ericsson Telephone Company. They

74. Ericsson Telephone Co. c.1905

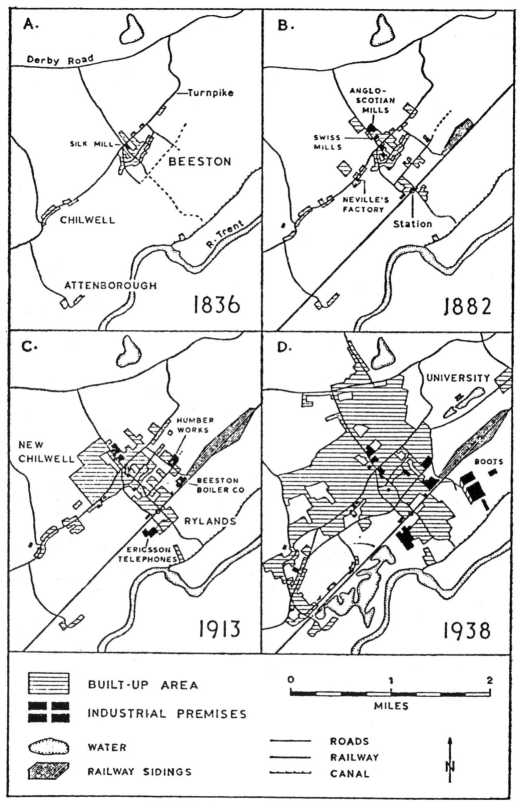

75. The Development of Beeston, 1836-1938

expanded greatly during the following years, and by 1916 employment had risen to over 1,000 workers and increased to over 4,500 by 1939, due to the demand for telephonic equipment world wide. In 1904 the Angular Hole Drilling and Manufacturing Co. set up its engineering works and as contractors for H.M. Government departments.

Alas, in 1907 there was a setback in the village's economy when the great Humber Company moved to Coventry, taking 3,000 workers with them. Fortunately, in 1908/9 three new firms came into the area: John Perry & Co. took over the Humber Mills for the production of hairnets, which could be made on the old Leaver type machines; F. W. Barnes & Sons Ltd. opened a branch factory in the Anglo-Scotian Mills for the production of lace furnishings and tablecloths. Finally in 1908, Sir Arthur Black purchased the Humber factory, which was later to be used for his plant of new machines to manufacture plain nets and mosquito nets, mainly for export. The former assembly shop was used to accommodate some of the newest machines of 274" width. By 1914 it had 42 machines and had increased to 118 by 1952, of whom 90 were accommodated in one shop. In addition, part of the extensive premises were let off to tenants, some of whom were lace makers.

About this time too, the hosiery industry had a small revival by the establishment of the firm of J. Barlow & Co. Ltd., which specialised in the manufacture of fancy half-hose and later diversified into the production of jumpers and cardigans, etc., continuing to thrive until very recent days.

World War I brought changes with many men on military service and women drafted to employment at the large shell filling factory at Chilwell.

76. Beeston Maltings

The 1920s brought new industries, especially light engineering and metal works firms such as Collingham & Owen, and Anglo-Scotian Electrical Engineering Works. Shaw & Marvin started their dyeing and finishing firm about this time and continued to expand. Several small lace and hosiery firms began, often renting 'standings' in the larger factories. The Beeston brewery, established as early as 1879, was acquired by Shipstones in 1926 and its maltings by the railway were enlarged.

The Nottingham Co-Operative Society opened their Hide & Skin Department, taking advantage of a site adjoining the railway. The existence of good railway communications with Nottingham and Derby and the presence of large areas of level land on the eastern side of the town close to the city have encouraged many of the more recent industrial developments. This has been especially true of the largest one: the arrival of the Boots Pure Drug Co. Ltd., which was to make a dramatic impact on the town.

2. The History of Boots the Chemists in Beeston

In 1919, Jesse Boot bought the large estate of Highfields, together with some adjoining land in Beeston which Jesse had envisaged to be used as an industrial village scheme. When this scheme became imprac-ticable, John Boot suggested that the land might be utilised for another of Jesse's visionary projects, to build a huge new manufacturing plant which would incorporate the very latest ideas of industrial production. Already at the Island Street and Station Street premises in Nottingham there was a severe shortage of space, so expansion would be impossible there and the land already bought at Beeston seemed to be a solution to the problem.

A planning committee was appointed to examine the site's development and a further 156 acres were bought in 1927. In 1928/9 the new soapworks were built there, designed by Hedley Jessop, Boot's engineer. This was to be followed by vast new factory buildings for the manufacture, storage and distribution of the 'wet' and 'dry' goods. Sir Owen Williams, a famous engineer, was engaged to design the 'wets' factory and he produced a most innovative plan of concrete and glass, which when built in 1933 was described as a "milestone in modern architecture". In 1938 came the building of the 'drys' factory, bringing even more workers into this industrial complex, which now extended to over 264 acres. Production increased as

77. Boots' 'Wets' Factory, 1934

the factories were "models of mechanised production" and with the outbreak of war in 1939 a considerable proportion of the factory's products were utilised by the Ministry of Supply and great quantities of important drugs and chemicals were turned out for this purpose.

The Company has always placed special emphasis on the health, recreation and well-being of its employees. An Industrial Health Unit is provided on site, giving the best medical care and attention at all times. Further education is also available for all employees in the Boots College and all workers under eighteen spend one day a week there. Sports facilities are included in the many benefits the company gives to its employees.

The firm's undertakings are so varied in character that they offer a wide range of skilled and unskilled employment for men and women, as well as professional, technical and managerial opportunities at all levels. So great is the available field of employment, that despite that proximity to Nottingham, the daytime population of Beeston substantially exceeds the residential population, as some people travel considerable distances to work in the town.

It is the ultimate aim of the Boots Company that all its various departments: manufacturing, distribution and research; shall be concentrated on the Beeston site and further land has been acquired for this purpose. Beeston is thus assured of its prime position as an industrial centre in the twenty-first century.

Social Changes

3. Local Government

The increased industrialisation of Beeston by the 1930s with the resultant residential expansion brought significant changes in Local Government. In 1933 the Urban District lost a small part of its territory on its eastern boundary under the Nottingham Extension Act. In 1935 it was decided to abolish the Stapleford Rural District Council and its area, including Chilwell, Attenborough and Toton as well as Stapleford was to be amalgamated

78. Town Hall, Foster Avenue

with Beeston to form the Beeston and Stapleford Urban District Council, with a population of 31,000 (by 1961, its population had increased to 56,560 and the Council became one of the largest Urban Districts in the country).

79. Beeston Library

The Council Offices in the Square proved inadequate for the enlarged membership and in 1938 the Town Hall was built on Foster Avenue.

Housing. In 1928 the Council bought land in the north east of the town from Sir Dennis Readett Bayley, Mr. C. Burrows and others to create the Beeston Fields housing estate, upon which 688 council houses and bungalows were erected. About the same time, land was acquired in the south of the town to form the Cliftonside estate on which a considerable number of houses were to be built during the later years.

Education. In 1931 Nottinghamshire County Council provided three new schools on the Beeston Fields estate: a secondary school for boys, a junior and an infants school. Later, a small school was built on the Cliftonside estate to accommodate infant and junior children there.

Library. In 1936/7 Nottinghamshire County Council provided a small branch library in shop premises on Station Road. On 21st April, 1938 the present library on Foster Avenue was opened and it fulfilled a great need for this area.

Health. A Maternity and Welfare Centre was established on Dovecote Lane.

80. Beeston Fire Station

81. Beeston Square and Boer War Memorial, c.1912

82. Beeston Square, 1970

83. Dovecote Lane Recreation Ground, c.1930

Fire Service. Around 1901 the Beeston Urban District Council built a new fire station in Stoney Street to replace old premises on Station Road, and provided more up-to-date equipment and later housing for fire officers there. In 1965 a more modern station was built on Station Road.

Transport is provided by:
a)   Railway from Beeston Station
b)   Road by buses operated until very recently by Barton Transport and by Nottingham City Transport since the 1920s.

84. Beeston Post Office

4. Commerce

Banking services increased and the Beeston branch of the Nottingham Joint Stock Bank moved to new premises in the Square in 1902, and in 1905 became the Midland Bank. Soon they were joined by a branch of Barclay's bank and in 1911 by the Westminster Bank.

The Nottingham Co-operative Society opened a large store on the High Road in 1900 with a branch on Queen's Road in 1907. A little later Boots opened a large shop built in Tudor style in the Square, which had its own Booklovers' Library.

The Post Office, formerly attached to a shop on the High Road, opened a new building in the Square early in the century, and in 1935 rebuilt on a site at the junction of Chilwell Road and Foster Avenue. Beeston had its own Building Society from 1883 and various other societies acquired premises here as interest in home ownership grew through the century.

5. Cultural Activities

Adult education classes were inaugurated in the evenings in local schools and continue today, generally through Broxtowe College. Since 1945, the Workers' Educational Association have organised classes in the library. Around 1903 Beeston produced its own newspaper, the 'Beeston Echo' which was later to be amalgamated with a rival 'Beeston Gazette' to form the 'Beeston Gazette and Echo'. This newspaper was eventually discontinued on 15th October, 1981.

85. Former Police Station (built c.1870)

86. Beeston Police Station

6. Religious Life

Has continued with churches of all the major denominations here. This century has also seen the advent of the Salvation Army and other evangelical and pentecostal churches.

7. Recreational Activities

In the early 1900s bee-keeping was a popular hobby, but it declined later. (The statue of the beekeeper on the High Road commemorates this.)

87. Roman Catholic Church, Foster Avenue

In 1908 the Council purchased land on Dovecote Lane for a Recreation Ground which was equipped by the Pearson family. Later, in 1923, Sir Louis Pearson gave land on Broadgate for a similar purpose and in the 1930s the Council designated land on Beeston Fields for recreation. As a result, there are flourishing rugby, hockey, football and cricket clubs as well as angling clubs.

Youth organisations have developed in the town from 1908 when the 17th Nottingham Boys' Brigade and Lads' Club was formed by S. H. Pearson and in 1909 the 1st Beeston Scout Troop and in 1916 the 1st Beeston Girl Guide Company. In 1949 a youth and community centre was opened in West End.

Entertainment was provided by two cinemas on the High Road: the Palace and the Palladium, and later by the Majestic on Queen's Road. Musical interests include Beeston Town Silver Band, formed in 1931; the Musical Society formed in 1946 and various choirs.

88. The Picture Palace, High Road, 1935

Post War Developments 1950-95

89. New Council Offices

1. Local Government

Beeston had become an Urban District by 1894 and in 1897 built its first Council offices on the site of the old pinfold (now the Square).

In 1974 the Beeston and Stapleford Urban District Council was enlarged to include parishes in the northern area ie. Awsworth, Brinsley, Cossall, Eastwood, Greasley, Kimberley, Nuthall and Strelley, and took on the new name of Broxtowe. This recalls the historical division of the county in Danish times known as the 'Broxtowe Wapentake'.

In 1977 the Council was given Borough status and the office of Mayor was established. The increased membership of the council (now 49) entailed the extension of the Town Hall to include a new Council Chamber. In the 1990s new Borough Offices were erected on Foster Avenue opposite the Town Hall to accommodate the many Borough Departments on one site.

2. Industrial and Social Affairs

In the 1950s came further industrial diversification with the addition of various engineering firms, particularly Sheerfabs Ltd. with its emphasis on welding and sheet metal work. The hosiery industry added a new dimension by the manufacture of nylon stockings at the firm of F. W. Sellors Ltd. Everlastic Ltd. started here for the making of ladies' support garments. A newcomer to the industrial scene was the glass making firm of F. Copley & Co.

New workers were brought into the town and thus created a demand for additional housing. The council and private firms responded and many houses and bungalows were built. At the same time, Round Hill Primary School was erected to cater for children in the north-west of the town.

90. Roundhill School, Foster Avenue

By the 1960s the increase of traffic, particularly through the High Road, was causing problems and forward planning was prepared for this area. The fire station on Stoney Street was too small for present needs and the demolition of some old property on Station Road (including the old National School) provided a larger area for a new fire station to be built there and equipped with more up-to-date appliances. This was opened in 1965.

The area around the Square was considered for development and the Second Covent Garden Property Co. Ltd. was approached. Eventually, old properties there and in Church Street and Chapel Street were demolished and the present shopping centre was built and opened in 1970.

The rise in the population of the town, particularly of the elderly, encouraged the County Council to build a residential home on Queen's Road East for those unable to care for themselves. This was called the Hassocks. In the later years (from 1979 onwards) there has been a continuing policy of building complexes of warden-aided flats, chiefly near the town centre. In many cases this has been achieved by the demolition of old property in Willoughby Street, Union Street, Middle Street, City Road and Acacia Walk.

By 1969-70 the traffic flow problem was acute and a ring road was make to the south of the High Road by extending Middle Street North westwards through the Vicarage land to Chilwell Road. At the same time, the High Road became one way in an easterly direction. During the same year, access to the south of the town was improved by a bridge over the railway to replace the old level crossing.

91. Sainsbury's Superstore

Car parks became imperative and various off street parks were designated in addition to the large multi-storey car park attached to the shopping centre. During the 1980s, the shopping centre was attracting large grocery and other stores, with the result that the smaller shops on the High Road were closing. Sainsbury's, who had earlier taken premises in the centre, decided in 1985 to take over a large area in Albion Street and Villa Street and build a superstore there. This caused the final demise of other small grocery shops, apart from the Co-op store (which closed in 1993) and Kwiksave store in the shopping centre. During 1985/6 the High Road was pedestrianised as far as Derby Street and Stoney Street became the access road to Sainsbury's.

The 1990s have brought further changes in industry. There are no hosiery firms here and only one small lace firm on Queen's Road East. What a change this is from the 1890s! One textile firm survives, making braids and fringes in a small factory off Wollaton Road. Above all, the Beeston Boiler Co, for so long one of the main employers of labour, was compelled to close in December 1985 and the whole works area has been given over to housing.

Fortunately, other firms have come in bringing a new slant to industry. One is the large Freight Container Terminal plant established conveniently near the railway on the site of the old creosote works. In line with current trends we have a number of small firms producing computers and their components. Light engineering firms, car and garage equipment firms have also come in, many taking over small units in the former Plessey (now GPT) land which has become a Technology Park.

92. Royal Mail Sorting Office

Boots are now the largest employer in the town. In 1995 they brought their remaining Nottingham based departments to new premises on the Beeston site, so at last fulfilling Sir Jesse Boot's dream for his works to be established here.

The very latest development has been the Royal Mail's new Nottingham District Sorting Office which has been built in Beeston on Padge Road. This was opened in 1995 and is now in full operation with the latest electronic equipment.

The rise of so many manufacturing firms has been complemented by an increase in commercial firms, banks and legal and accountancy businesses. Many of these have settled in and around the High Road, which has really become a commercial centre rather than a shopping area – alas!

3. Cultural Life

Although Nottingham University is within the city boundary, it is very close to Beeston and some of its student accommodation is here. Since the expansion of the University, especially during the last twenty years, an increasing number of the University staff have taken up residence here and have contributed greatly to the cultural life here. The advent of Broxtowe College in neighbouring Chilwell has also brought many academic people into the town. New societies have come into being since 1950, especially the Civic Society and the Local History Society. There has been an increase in Further Education and W.E.A. classes in a variety of subjects.

93. 'Octagons' – University Student Accommodation

A great achievement has been our partnership in Europe, in which we have become twinned with Gutersloh in Germany. This was inaugurated in 1978 and through the years since then, strong links have been forged by groups in the two communities to our mutual benefit and friendship. We owe special thanks to the Broxtowe Twinning Association for this venture.

Our knowledge has been broadened too by the many new residents from overseas whom we have been happy to welcome into our community.

Recreational activities continue to be provided and in greater variety but often outside the town itself: for example, swimming at Bramcote Baths; badminton etc. at Chilwell Olympia. Entertainment is no longer provided by the cinemas and dance halls. All have closed. Concerts are given in church halls or at the University. The Operatic Society performs in Nottingham. Many people now prefer home entertainment through television or videos.

The wide range of activities and interests which have proliferated through this century in the town (of which the aforementioned are but a few) is indicative of the lively and enthusiastic community who, through the centuries, have welcomed strangers who have become part of the Beeston family. Long may this continue!

94. Beeston's 'Beekeeper' Sculpture, High Road

Conclusion

The Beeston which I have known and loved is fast disappearing. Future generations will no longer be able to walk through the Twitchell in Round Hill field, or wander through the Robinets collecting frog spawn or watercress from the Pasture Dyke, nor can they paddle in the Tottle Brook and fill their bottles with its water to soothe sore eyes. Once it was always interesting to walk along the High Road with its variety of small shops, each vying with the other for your custom and all ready to offer their services.

Fortunately, a little of this heritage is being preserved in the West End Conservation Area where the Manor House, the Old Manor House and the other seventeenth and eighteenth century houses are situated. In addition, we intend to retain the best of the early twentieth century houses in the St. John's Grove Preservation Area around Devonshire Avenue and Elm Avenue.

It is my fervent hope that the young people of today will endeavour to keep these reminders of our past history which have shaped Beeston's distinctive character.

95. Above: The Old Manor House (c.1685)
96. Above Right: West End Cottage (c.1601)
97. Below Right: West End House (c.1560)

Appendix One

Lords of the Manor of Beeston 1066-1537

Pre 1066	Alfag, Alwine & Ulchel (and one soc man)
11067/8 - 1113	William Peveril I – granted by William I
1113-49	William Peveril II
1149-54	William Peveril III - disinherited for conspiracy and support for Stephen
1154-1171	The Crown – Henry II
1171	Beeston divided into two Manors:

The Beauchamp Manor

1171-1216	Hugh de Beauchamp of Eaton Socan, Bedfordshire
1216-35	Roger de Beauchamp
1235-42	Miles de Beauchamp and Richard de Beauchamp
1242-50	Miles de Beauchamp and John de Beauchamp
1250	William de Beauchamp
After 1250	Richard de Beauchamp II and Hugh de Beauchamp III Isabel and Matilda de Beauchamp
1275	Sarah de Walton (grand daughter of Richard de Beauchamp II)
1280	Sarah de Walton now de Hockenwold
1284	Ralph de Beauchamp
c1300	Roger de Beauchamp II
1348	Roger de Beauchamp III and descendants of the Beauchamp family and Sarah de Walton to:
1523	Lord John Hussey of Sleaford
1536	Lord John Hussey executed (Pilgrimage of Grace)
1536-60	The Crown

Appendix Two

The Monastic Manor

Priors of Wymondley 1200-1537 and Lords of the Manor of Beeston

William	c1218
Hugh	1233-4
Martin	1246 – died 1247/8
Richard de Waldia	elected 1247/8
John de Marden	resigned 1290
John de Wymondley	elected 1290 - deprived 1300
John de Marden	re-elected 1300 - died 1304
Elias de Wheathamstead	elected 1304 – died 1340
John de Buckden	elected 1340 - resigned 1345 - died 1347
William Legat	elected 1345 – died 1349
Roger de Beeston	elected 1349 – resigned 1374
John Anabull	resigned 1404/5
John Stevens	instituted 1404/5
Richard Chapman	instituted 1442
John Bawdry	died 1478
William Hawes/Howes	elected 1478 – resigned 1513
Robert Ellis	elected 1513 – resigned 1520
William Weston	elected 1520 – died 1531
John Dorchester	elected 1531
John Atue or Yate	elected 1537 – Priory suppressed

Appendix Three

Vicars of Beeston c1200-1485

c1200	Robert – a Chaplain	1420	John Thimbelby
c1240	Roger	1423	John Gynger
1267	John de Brademore		Thomas Smith
1275	Matthew de Leycestre	1431	John Katull
1327	William de Willesthorpe	1451	John Meyson
1339	William de Beckford		John Emott
1349	Thomas Fitzroger de Oxton	1455	Nicholas Bubwith
1376	William Askham	1456	William Taylor
	Richard Mason		Richard Ellesley
1401	Henry Serle	1465	Nicholas Blackwell
1405	Thomas Marchall		

Appendix Four

INQUISITIONES POST MORTEM: WM. DE BESTON 1353/4

Writ dated at Westminster 26 Jan. 28 Edw. III [1353/4]

INQUISITION taken at Nottingham on the Monday after the feast of St. Valentine 28 Edw. III [17 Feb. 1353/4] before *John Waleys* Escheator for the county of Nottingham, by the oath of *William de Whorthyngton*, *Robert Casteltayn* of Bramcote, *William* son of *Richard de Beston*, *William Maunchester*, *John de Beston*, *John* son of *John* the same, *Wiliam Warde* of Trowell, *Robert de Dylwastre* of the same, *John Glasinwryth* of Lenton, *Robert de Rolke*, *John Cargetter* of Lenton and *John Serle* of the same who say that _William de Beston_ parson of the church of Cotegrave holds two messuages and a virgate of land in Beston which were formerly held by *Maud Rogers* of Beston and *Hugh Master Husone* of the same, and one virgate in Beston which *Robert de Casteltayn* of Bramcote and *Margaret* his wife hold in Beston of the aforesaid *William* for term of the life of the said *Margaret* by the gift of the said *William* held of *Roger de Bello Campo* by the service of the 20th part of a knight's fee for all services – worth 8*s* 8*d* a year.

And they say that *William de Beston* holds a messuage and the moiety of a virgate of land in Beston formerly held by *John de Strelleye* of Nottingham of *William de Maunchester* of Beston and *Alice de Langton* of the same by the service of 5*s* yearly, they hold the same of *Roger de Bello Campo* by the service of the 50th part of a knight's fee and the same *Roger* hold the same messuage, &c., and others in Beston of the King in chief. The said messuage and moiety of a virgate are worth 3*s* 4*d* a year. The same _William de Beston_ holds 2 messuages and 34 acres of land in Lenton which were held by *John de Tombys* of Nottingham and a piece of meadow containing 4 acres called Doddesholm of the Prior of Lenton by the service of 7*s* 6*d* a year, the 2 messuages and 34 acres are worth 20*s* a year and the piece of meadow 8*s*.

The said Prior holds the same of the King as of his honour of Peverell in pure and perpetual alms. It is not to the loss of prejudice of the King or of any other if the said _William de Beston_ gives or assigns the lands and tenements mentioned in the writ to a certain chaplain and his successors.

[*C.* 143/314/16]

Appendix Five

Livings and Pensions of Chantry Priests

Parish	Chantry, Guild, etc.	I Edward VI 1547–8					2-3 Philip and Mary 1555–6			
		Name of Priest	Age	Valuation			Name of Priest	Pension		
				£	s.	d.		£	s.	d.
Annesley	Sir Wm. Wakebridge's and Robt. Annesley's Chantry,	Edmund Garnett	48	5	9	11½	Edmund Garnet	5	0	0
Beeston	St. Katherine's Chantry	Alexander Constable	40	4	9	2	Alexander Constable	4	0	3
Bingham	Our Lady's Guild	William Cranswyke	52	5	2	9	William Cranswicke	4	0	0
Blyth	Stipendiary Service	Thomas Twellys	56	3	1	10	Thomas Twelles	2	15	0
Caunton	Our Lady's Chantry	Richard Stanshall	50	4	8	8	Richard Stanshall	4	0	0
Clifton	Holy Trinity College	John Fynes (Warden)	76				John Fynes	6	0	0
		Thomas Wright	50	21	5	9	Thomas Wrighte	5	0	0
		Thomas Bowthe	76				Thomas Bothe	5	0	0
Clifton, North	Harby Chantry	Thomas Belyalde	50	5	0	0	Thomas Behald	4	0	0
Coddington	St. Peter's Chantry	Edmund Norman	63	5	12	8	Edward Norman	5	0	0
Edwinstowe	Clipstone Chantry	John Thomson	48	5	0	0	John Thompsonne	4	0	0
Gonalston	Brodbusk Hospital	Thomas Newenton	60	5	18	9	Thomas Newenton	5	0	0

Appendix Six

Plague Victims 1593–4

John and Joan Reckless and 5 children
John and Elizabeth James and 4 children
Elizabeth Levis and 3 children
Isabel Levis and 2 children
John and Joan Wragg and 3 children
7 members of the Waplington family
4 members of the Bailey family
4 members of the Shrigley family
5 members of the Ward family
6 members of the Brown family
4 members of the Oliver family
3 members of the Willimott family
3 members of the Jellibrand family
3 members of the Fowkes family
3 members of the Smalley family
3 members of the Spenser family
3 members of the Raby family
Elizabeth and Eliza Adenburrow

William and Katherine Outram
William and Agnes Taylor
John and Robert Henson
Thos. and Richard Booth
Thos. and William Gandie
Isabel and Robert Bampton
Margaret and Thos. Griffin
Alice and Marie Raven
Margaret and Wm. Lacey
William, Joan and Nicholas Hall
Marlin and Richard Chambers
Jane and Agnes Mee
John and Elizabeth Steel
Jane Courtney
Dorothy Taylor
Joan Moore
Henry Richards
Henry Pearson

Henry Parnell
John and Widow Morris
Elizabeth Butler
Richard Dolphin
John Doar
George Widdowson
William Constable
Dorothy Patterson
Antony Smith
Alice Hill
Humphrey Tomlinson
Margaret Roberts
Mary Patrick
Robert Reynolds
Thomas Arnold
John Vicars
Marie Harlshom

Appendix Seven

Protestation Returns — Beeston

Apart from very few entries in the Parish Registers during the Civil War, there are no marriages recorded from 1643 to 1653.

Aram, George
Attenborough, William
Bingham, Thomas
Booth, John
Booth, Richard
Bostock, Robert
Bostocke, George
Bostocke, Gervas
Bostocke, Robert jun
Burges, Jervas
Calver, Francis
Calvery, Francis
Chambers, Henry
Constable, Gervis (Overseer)
Constable, John
Constable, William
Cooke, Gabriel
Day, William
Dickinson, William
Gadsbie, Swillington
German, Thomas
Hall, Robert
Heb, William
Heb, Robert

Henson, Thomas
Hooton, Nicholas
James, Nicholas
James, Thomas
Johnson, Gervas
Kindersley, Walter (Vicar)
Kirkbie, John
Kirkbie, William
Lacie, Richard
Lacie, Richard jun
Lacie, Thomas
Lacie, Thomas
Lacie, Thomas
Lacie, William
Lambert, William
Levis, William (Overseer)
Levis, William
Levis, William
Marshall, John
Martin, Edward
Moore, Henry
Morrice, Nicholas
Phippes, John
Pierson, Bartholomew

Rawlinson, William
Robberts, Raph
Rockett, John Curate
Ryder, Richard
Sandes, John
Scot, Richard
Scot, Richard
Smalley, Henry
(Church Mester)
Smalley, Robert
(Church Mester)
Smalley, William
Smith, John
Smith, Raph
Smith, Thomas
Smith, William
Sregley (or Shrigley)
Anthony (Constable)
Steevens, William
Stonesbie, Francis
Strey, Nicholas
Stringer, Richard
Stringer, Thomas
Tinsley, Anthony

Toplay, Richard
Turpin, George
Turpin, John
Turpin, Nicholas
Turpin, Thomas
Turpin, Thomas
Turpine, Richard
Upton, George
Waplington, Henry
Waplington, Henry
Waplington, Henry jun
Waplinton, John
Waplinton, Richard
Waplinton, Thomas
West, George
West, William
Weston, John
Wilde, Humphrey
Williamson, George
Willimat, Reynald
Winfield, William
Wright, William

Appendix Eight

Obituary of Timothy Wylde from 'The Nottingham Journal', 1st February 1799

"On Saturday last*, at his home on the High-pavement in this town, at the great age of 93, the Rev Timothy Wylde, rector of Beeston, in this neighbourhood, and vicar of Winkfield, in Berkshire. He was elected headmaster of the Free Grammar-School in Stoney-street, in the year 1758; from which situation he retired a few years since. He retained all his faculties till within a day or two prior to his dissolution. Wednesday his remains were interred in St. Peter's church".

* Saturday 26 January 1799.

Appendix Nine

Table 1
Occupations of the Population of Beeston Parish, 1851

Agriculture 93

Mining 1

Manufacturing 1,259
    Lace making 282
    Lace mending, etc. 114
    Framework knitting 186
    Hosiery seaming, stitching, etc. 52
    Silk 377
    Cotton 24
    Clothing 119
    Engineering and metal goods 47
    Other manufacturing industries 58

Services 275
    Retail distribution 45
    Personal service 167
    Professional services 31
    Other services 32

Labourers (undefined) 42

TOTAL IN OCCUPATION 1,670

Source: *1851 Census Enumeration Schedules, Public Records Office, H.O. 107/2127.*

Table 2
Number of Manufacturers in Selected Industries in Beeston, 1864–1958

	Lace Industry			Hosiery Industry			Engineering Industries		
	Lace	Curtains & Net	Total	Hosiery	Shawls etc.	Total	Metals & Engineering	Cycles	Total
1864	13	—	13	—	—	—	—	—	—
1876	14	—	14	4	1	5	1	—	1
1881	13	1	14	2	2	4	1	1	2
1891	27	2	29	1	2	3	2	1	3
1899	18	2	20	—	2	2	1	4	5
1912	24	9	33	3	1	4	7	2	9
1922	17	15	32	2	2	4	6	1	7
1936	14	6	20	4	2	6	10	1	11
1958	5	4	9	6	1	7	13	—	13

Sources: *Kelly's Directories of Nottinghamshire, 1864–1936.*
    H.M. Factory Inspectorate, Nottingham District Registers (1958).

Table 3
Occupations of the Population of Beeston, 1901–1931

	1901		1911		1921		1931	
	No.	%	No.	%	No.	%	No.	%
Agriculture	**101**	**3**	**145**	**3**	**147**	**3**	**145**	**2**
Mining and Quarrying	**45**	**1**	**68**	**1**	**72**	**1**	**31**	**—**
Manufacturing	**1,960**	**59**	**2,779**	**56**	**2,771**	**52**	**3,445**	**49**
Engineering and Metal Goods	514	15	985	20	1,243	23	1,559	22
Textiles	1,193	36	1,287	26	909	17	994	14
Clothing	190	6	258	5	253	5	348	5
Other Manufacturing Industries	63	2	249	5	366	7	554	8
Services	**1,162**	**37**	**1,975**	**40**	**2,387**	**44**	**3,514**	**49**
Other Occupations	658		225		372		597	
Total Occupied	**3,926**		**5,292**		**5,749**		**7,732**	

Notes: The percentage figures refer to percentage of total occupied excluding those in "other occupations".

Sources: *Census of England and Wales, Nottinghamshire, Occupational returns for Beeston U.D., 1901, 1911, 1921, Occupation Tables, 1931.*

Table 4
Number of Insured Employees in Beeston Labour Exchange Area, 1948–58

	1948		1953		1958	
	No.	%	No.	%	No.	%
Agriculture } **Mining and Quarrying** }	**214**	**1**	**212**	**1**	**180**	**1**
Manufacturing	**12,094**	**55**	**13,584**	**65**	**14,911**	**66**
Engineering and Metals	6,096	28	7,803	37	9,233	41
Textiles	1,356	6	1,395	7	1,279	5
Clothing	252	1	399	2	366	2
Other Manufacturing Industries	4,390	20	3,987	19	4,033	17
Services	**9,401**	**44**	**6,970**	**34**	**7,433**	**33**
National & local government	5,580	25	4,231	20	3,825	17
Other Services	3,821	19	2,741	14	3,608	16
Total	**21,709**		**20,766**		**22,524**	

Notes: The Employment Exchange Area includes Beeston, Chilwell, Bramcote and Attenborough, but not Stapleford and Toton.

Sources: Ministry of Labour, North Midlands Regional Office.

Bibliography

Chapter 2

F. M. Stenton, *Anglo-Saxon England*
Robert Mellors, *In and About Nottinghamshire*
Arthur Cossons, *Beeston and Stapleford Guide*

Chapter 3

Domesday Book entry
Accounts Roll 1297
David Rolfe, *Pre-Conquest Predecessors in Nottinghamshire*
Arthur Cossons, *Lecture notes*
Thoroton, *History of Nottinghamshire*
Godfrey, *History of the Parish and Priory of Lenton*
Court Rolls 1154 re Beeston
Honour of Peveril
Mellors, *In and About Nottinghamshire*
Holland Walker, *Links with Old Nottingham*

Chapter 6

Perry Williams, *Life in Tudor England*

Chapter 7

Arthur Cossons, *Early Enclosures*
Tithe Award Map 1806/9
A.C. Wood, *History of Nottinghamshire*, pp.172-194
Wedgewood, *The King's War and the King's Peace*
Protestation Returns 1642
Memoirs of Col. Hutchinson
Parish Registers
Rentals for Toton 1644, Nottingham Archive Office
The Beeston Canal, City of Nottingham publication
W. Felkin, *History of the Hosiery and Lace Industry*
Parish Registers: 1698, 1700-1740, 1750, Nottingham Archives Office
Quarter Sessions Records, 1795, Nottingham Archives Office

Illustrations

Illustrations for this publication have been provided by the following:

Local Studies Library, Angel Row: Nos. 20, 22, 53, 58, 72, 73, 74, 77, 81, 88

Nottinghamshire Archives: No. 36

Nottingham Castle Museum: No. 6

Margaret Cooper: Nos. 13, 35, 54, 68, 70, 82, 83

© Ian Brown, LRPS: Nos. 24, 29, 32, 40-43, 45, 50, 51, 56, 57, 59, 60, 62, 63, 65, 76, 78-80, 84-87, 89-97

Front Cover: Beeston Canal
Anglo-Scotian Mills, Wollaton Road
Beeston Manor House, Middle Street
Beekeeper Sculpture by Siobhan Coppinger, High Road
(©Photographs by Ian Brown, LRPS)

Back Cover: Engraving of the Church of St. John the Baptist, after its rebuilding in 1844 by Scott and Moffatt.

ISBN 0 900943 89 0

Published by Nottinghamshire County Council
Typeset and printed by Central Print Services
County Hall, West Bridgford, Nottingham NG2 7QP

Nottinghamshire County Council
Leisure Services